LIVING OUT LOUD

LIVING OUT LOUD

Conversations about virtue, ethics, and evangelicalism

Stanley Hauerwas, Samuel Wells and friends

edited by Luke Bretherton and Russell Rook

Paternoster:
thinking faith

16 15 14 13 12 11 10   7 6 5 4 3 2 1

First published 2010 by Paternoster
Paternoster is an imprint of Authentic Media Limited
Milton Keynes
www.authenticmedia.co.uk/paternoster

British Library Cataloguing in Publication Data

A catalogue record for this book is available from the
British Library

ISBN 978-1-84227-720-1

Cover design by David Smart
Printed and bound in Great Britain by Bell and Bain, Glasgow

Acknowledgements

We would like to especially thank Brianna Stynes L'Hostis for all her help in putting this book together. Her contribution was invaluable. We would also like to thank Sam and Jo Bailey Wells for their generous hospitality in hosting the participants in the roundtable discussion that form such a central part of this book. In addition we are grateful to Steve Chalke and Shane Claiborne for setting aside the time to talk, and to Carole Baker and Emily Wilson-Hauger at Duke University for their help with the finer details. Thanks go to Alan Johnson, Wendy Beech-Ward, and the Spring Harvest Theme Group for their support, and to Matt Little for his work during the early days of this project. None of this would have been possible were it not for Robin Parry at Paternoster and his constant encouragement and expertise. We are particularly indebted to Sam Wells and Stanley Hauerwas for inspiring us, enabling the project to be undertaken, and agreeing to take part.

Permissions

Chapter 2 was originally published as 'Theology as Narrative' in Samuel Wells, *Improvisation: The Drama of Christian Ethics* (Grand Rapids: Brazos, 2004), chapter 2. Reproduced here by kind permission from Brazos Press.

Chapter 3 was originally published as 'The Politics of Church: How We Lay Bricks and Make Disciples' in Stanley Hauerwas, *After Christendom?: How the Church is to Behave if Freedom, Justice and a Christian Nation are Bad Ideas* (Nashville: Abingdon, 1991), chapter 4. Reproduced here with kind permission from Stanley Hauerwas.

Chapter 4 was originally published as 'Carving Stone or Learning to Speak Christian' in Stanley Hauerwas, *The State of the University: Academic Knowledges and the Knowledge of God* (Malden, MA: Blackwell, 2007), chapter 7. Reproduced here with kind permission from Stanley Hauerwas.

Chapter 5 was originally published as 'On Developing Hopeful Virtue' in Stanley Hauerwas and Charles Pinches, *Christians Among the Virtues: Theological Conversations with Ancient and Modern Ethics* (Notre Dame, IN: University of Notre Dame Press, 1997), chapter 7. Reproduced here with kind permission from Stanley Hauerwas.

Chapter 6 was originally published as 'The Servant Community: Christian Social Ethics' in Stanley Hauerwas, *The Peaceable Kingdom: A Primer in Christian Ethics* (Notre Dame, IN: University of Notre Dame Press, 1983). Reproduced here with kind permission from Stanley Hauerwas.

Chapter 7 was originally published as Samuel Wells 'How Common Worship Forms Local Character', *Studies in Christian Ethics* 15:1 (2002): 66–74. Reproduced here by kind permission from SAGE Publications.

Chapter 9 was originally published as 'Sex in Public: How Adventurous Christians are Doing it' in Stanley Hauerwas, *A Community of Character: Toward a Constructive Christian Social Ethic* (Notre Dame, IN: University of Notre Dame Press, 1981), chapter 10. Reproduced here with kind permission from Stanley Hauerwas.

Contents

Introduction

Luke Bretherton and Russell Rook

More of a conversation than a collection

I once attended an event advertised as 'more of a conversation than a conference.' It was some years ago yet I still remember the strap-line for two reasons. Firstly, I recall the quality of the conference, the quality of ideas and conversation – for once the experience lived up to the advertising. Secondly, it taught me a simple truth of how thinkers, leaders, and communicators best serve the church – part of our job is to share ideas and stimulate great conversations.

Living Out Loud takes the form of a conversation on a number of different levels. It is a conversation about what it means to be a disciple in the world that we live in. It is a conversation between theologians, church leaders, and Christians who are equipping the church for action. It is a conversation between you the reader and our contributors who have generously shared their thoughts, experiences, ministries, and message in this volume. Above all it is a conversation about Christian ethics.

This particular conversation began during the preparations for Spring Harvest. For those unaware, Spring Harvest is Europe's largest Christian conference attended by around 40,000 Christians who come together for a week of worship and teaching around Easter time. Over the last years Spring Harvest has sought to stimulate a range of vital conversations about Christian faith and theology in contemporary life. In particular, the plan was to make the 2010 event address the theme of ethics and explore what it means to live a Christian life in the twenty-first century.

In certain company, the thought of a prolonged conversation about Christian ethics is akin to a cure for insomnia. Some feel that we have heard it all before and that another round of well rehearsed arguments can only bore or frustrate. That said, few would doubt the central importance of ethics in Christian living. This book is an attempt at initiating a conversation among evangelicals so that a more dynamic approach to talking about and living out the moral life may emerge.

Rather than rehearsing tired or overly familiar conversations, we are seeking to engage in a different dialogue. By combining new ideas and ancient wisdom, activists and thinkers, theologians and ministers, we hope to reframe some of the conversations about Christian ethics. In particular we are looking to one model to provide fresh insight and ideas.

The American theologian, Stanley Hauerwas has long been recognised as a leading voice on the subject of Christian ethics. Over many years now his work has enabled Christians to take a fresh look at a familiar subject. Hauerwas' pioneering approach is commonly referred to as 'virtue ethics'. In this collection we have gathered essays by both Hauerwas and his long-term collaborator Sam Wells. These pieces outline some of the central themes of virtue ethics and help us to explore their implications for Christian discipleship and church life. The first section of the book explores virtue ethics as a way of 'doing' Christian ethics while the second section sets out some of the implications of virtue ethics for a number of concrete moral issues or questions.

The virtues in the Christian tradition

While virtue ethics has the potential to foster a new conversation within evangelicalism, it soon becomes obvious that its themes and approaches are deeply rooted in the Christian tradition.

In Christianity, the ultimate end or goal of human life, that which governs and determines our vision of what the truly good life entails, is communion with God and neighbour. But how might we fulfil this goal in the light of our understanding of what it means to be human (i.e. that we are created good, but fallen, and stand in need of redemption)? The language of virtue ethics is one of the main ways in which Christianity has framed its understanding of the habits of heart and personal dispositions necessary to achieve this end. In turn, this understanding enables us to move into ever deeper communion with God and neighbour through giving a godly or righteous shape to our life and actions. The language of virtues is a way of describing how we become what we do. Each action and gesture has consequences for our personal and moral formation as humans and hence shapes our ability to enter into communion with God and neighbour.

Understanding the interconnectedness of the ability to lead a good life and the ability to lead a virtuous life originated with Greek philosophy, in particular Plato, Aristotle, and the Stoics. They developed the notion that the basic human virtues were *temperance, courage* (or fortitude), *prudence* (or practical wisdom/rationality: i.e. knowledge of the appropriate action through reflection on experience) and *justice*. These virtues were called the cardinal virtues (from the Latin *cardo*, meaning 'hinge', as they were seen as pivotal to fulfilling the truly good life, the life of human flourishing). From very early on, one could say from the Epistles onwards, the church adopted the language of the virtues. However, it was not until the medieval period, notably in the work of the twelfth century theologian Thomas Aquinas, that the church developed more systematic treatments of virtue as a way of framing the moral life. Drawing on Scripture, Christianity added the theological virtues of *faith, hope,* and *love* to the basic list of 'cardinal' virtues.

Taking up and working with the language of the virtues as a way of talking about how to fulfil a Christian vision of the good life was a way of recognising the need to match belief and behaviour through concrete action. For example, a healthy person eats and enjoys food and through practicing temperance is neither anorexic nor obese. Acting well requires developing appropriate virtues, appropriate ways of behaving that enable us to think clearly about the right way to act. For example, if I decide to walk to church and have made sufficient preparation by leaving enough time, wearing appropriate clothes, finding out an interesting or quiet route, and so on, I am a prudent person. If I decide to walk but don't know the way, get soaking wet because I didn't bring a coat or umbrella, and am late because I didn't leave enough time, I am a imprudent person. My imprudence probably stems from other character flaws: I am impatient, or reckless, etc. Virtue ethics encapsulates the idea that my ability to make good decisions is directly related to the on-going practices, behaviours, and habits that I live out. Practising the virtues is literally a way of *living the gospel out loud.*

When we think about moral actions in terms of the virtues, we understand that making moral decisions involves the whole person. Ethics is not just a question of abstract reasoning, intelligence, or of knowing a great deal. Nor is it about making the right decision at a point of crisis. Rather, ethics involves the formation of persons who have the right priorities and develop the right virtues. Becoming a moral person has as much to do with the quality of our relationships and of our behaviour as it has to do with what we do or don't know or the decisions we do or don't make. Unless I am well nurtured and so learn how to love, how to be patient, how to restrain my anger or lust, I will not develop into the kind of person who has the necessary virtues to make good and wise decisions. For example, when deciding whether or not to have an abortion, a woman must have a certain knowledge of biology and the technical processes involved in having an abortion. But any decision made will involve certain virtues like courage, justice, love, and vices such as anger and despair. A decision will need to take into account other people: the foetus, family, friends, medical staff, and others. No decision can be centred on the needs and goals of the individual alone, but must be attentive to how others will be affected. Justice—the ability to give to each what is appropriately their due—is the centre of the cardinal virtues. Justice enables the formation of a community in which the flourishing of each individual is related to the flourishing of all.

For Christians, the cardinal virtues are never enough. However much we practice the virtues, we never overcome our sinful state and can never fulfil the fullness of our humanity. This is only given in Christ. Through the Holy Spirit we receive the gifts of faith, hope, and love. These gifts enable us to escape being wholly bound by sin and allow us to enter into communion with God. Through our encounter and relationship with God we receive faith (the knowledge of God), hope (an openness to and expectation of the new heaven and new earth and so an ability to act in such a way that the sinful world does not define the limits of reality and possibility), and love (our becoming more forgiving, generous, and loving through God's forgiveness, generosity, and love of us). Acting faithfully, hopefully, and lovingly show how God has acted upon us and changed us. They are the virtues that perfect our human ability and capacities. Unlike the cardinal virtues they do not arise through our relationships with other humans but only through our relationship with God and so are not a fruit of human power or work but divine power (or what we tend to call 'salvation' and 'sanctification').

In Catholic theology talk of virtue fell into disuse, as the emphasis was more on moral obligation, rules, and duty. Catholic moral theology focused on developing handbooks for confessors that could act as guides to the penitent. This tended to end up with a narrow moralism or legalism. For Protestants, from the Reformation period on, the emphasis was the centrality of grace and less on the kind of person we needed to be in order to act in such a way that we fulfilled what it meant to be human. As long as we heard the good news, the virtuous life would either somehow spontaneously follow on or was not necessary because we were already saved, and that was what really mattered. But the problem with this approach is what Dietrich Bonhoeffer called 'cheap grace'; grace has no transformative impact upon human life for it lacks a relationship with discipleship. Therefore, Christians have lost any sense of what the resurrection life entails. In recognition of the problems of moralism and cheap grace, talk of the virtues has come back into discussions of moral agency and action. The language of virtues is now being used by both Catholic and Protestant thinkers.

This book is meant as a contribution to the broadening conversation among evangelicals about how a virtue approach might help frame moral action. The essays by Hauerwas and Wells contained within the collection, and the conversations that precede and follows them, are devoted to exploring the implications of virtue ethics for Christian thought and living.

Joining the conversation

In seeking to facilitate a conversation rather than simply editing a collection we have chosen to introduce and intersect the various essays and chapters by Hauerwas and Wells with a series of conversations with other thinkers and communicators.

This book first came to life when Steve Chalke, Shane Claiborne, Jo Bailey Wells, and we joined Stanley Hauerwas and Sam Wells for two days of dialogue at Duke University in the August of 2009. It was a privilege for us, the editors, to facilitate these conversations and discuss the implications of virtue ethics for evangelical Christians and churches. These discussions help to frame the chapters of this book and provide insight into the out-working of these ideas in church life and Christian living.

The time has now come to invite you, the reader, to join the dialogue. We hope that you find the ideas stimulating and the dialogue enlivening. We hope that you join the conversation as you read, think, and act. As such we hope that this book will be a conversation starter for enquiring disciples who aspire to faithful Christian belief and practice.

Advent 2009

Chapter 1

Roundtable on Evangelicalism and Virtue Ethics 1[1]

Jo Bailey Wells, Luke Bretherton, Steve Chalke,
Shane Claiborne, Stanley Hauerwas, Russell Rook,
Samuel Wells

Steve Chalke:
This conversation is born out of a sense that there has been a massive loss of confidence among evangelicals and other Christians about what they believe and why they believe it. It's a loss of confidence that I think typically results in two responses: One group of people adopt the 'grin and bear it' approach. So they sit in the pew on Sunday; they go to the celebration; they stick their hands in the air—they go through the motions on the outside, but on the inside they are losing it. They have huge unanswered—indeed, many of them believe

unanswerable—questions about the way their faith relates to the rest of the world and their life experience. They live in two different worlds and struggle to bring the two together.

For example, I sat with a young man in his mid twenties, just two weeks ago, who said exactly that to me. He was doing a PhD in astrophysics at Cambridge and also attending a local evangelical church there. His comment was this: 'These two institutions, of which I am part, occupy different universes. I can't seem to bring them together.' But he didn't want to give up one or the other. My theory is that as the years go by, he will give up one. Probably the church.

The second response comes from the kind of person that tradition holds less power over. Instead of living with ambiguity, they just dump the church. One of the symptoms of this in the UK is the 'revolving door' syndrome: Masses of new people in, and masses of people out, all the time. Only this accounts for the mystery of the church that is always growing but never grows. There is a constant stream of new people, but there's always the same number of people, because the people are leaving as quickly as they are arriving. This is even true of some of our biggest churches—they provide a buzz and a kick, the band's great, and so on; but when you get beyond the lights, down to the meat of the thing, there's little substance—it's just not satisfying nor sustaining.

This is why it is vital that the church deals with the relationship between 'living a Christian life' and 'believing the Christian faith'. We've reduced ethics to those big quandaries: Should we go to war or not? Do we invest in this kind of medical science or not? What about assisted dying? For most of us ethics is about dealing with those tough issues. And we see the Bible as a rule book which prescribes the answers we need. However, the problem is that it just doesn't cover all the rules we need, it seems to be of no direct help with many of the moral dilemmas that life in the twenty first century throws at us.

Luke Bretherton:
Steve, do you want to say a bit more about the way moral questions are addressed and how you think churches deal with those hot button issues like same sex relationships, or abortion, or whatever. How is ethics done? How do you think people formulate their responses?

Steve Chalke:
There are a number of set public moral positions which Christians tend to buy 'off the shelf'. We tow the party line. In

that sense, I don't think that people formulate at all. But though they have these 'public' positions around hot potato moral issues, 'privately' they often hold different views and are asking endless, deeper questions: 'Does this fit?' 'Does it work?' 'How?' And though they are told what the Bible says and they've even read some verses about, for instance, the practice of homosexuality being wrong, they also know that the Bible appears to endorse slavery. And so, they're trying to work out on what basis we believe *this* bit of the Bible and not *that* bit of the Bible, and why we hang on to the verses in Leviticus that condemn homosexuality, yet dump the verses around them about a number of other categories of people who's situation in life (e.g. disability) or practices (e.g. wearing clothing made of the wrong materials) equally condemn them.

Russell Rook:
My own tradition has a classic 'positional' view which is fairly common among British evangelicalism. If you go to my denomination's website, you will find a banner on the front page that says 'What we believe'. If you trace your cursor across 'What we believe', a whole list of 'positional statements' will come down. If you want to know what we believe about war or what we believe about the sacraments, we have a positional statement for it. Despite the irony in the naming, we even have a positional statement on homosexuality.

There is this sense: 'Please tell us what to believe around this issue and then we will go and believe it, or at least we will *say* we believe it.' Stan, I read one of your essays in which you drew a comparison between the Aristot-elian disciples and the Stoics. The Aristotelian disciples were determined to take on the virtues and live them out in order to make them part of their identity, whereas the Stoics were determined to make the virtues part of their procedures in life and part of their self-presentation.

Evangelicals in the UK I think are similar to the Stoics. Many have a 'positional statement' on a number of ethical issues. Whether the position makes sense to them internally and whether they practice it is another issue altogether. What happens all too easily is they end up in a vicious circle where their faith is continually undermined by their life in the world; what they believe just doesn't square with their human experience and so they believe it less on the inside even if they continue to confess it on the outside.

Jo Bailey Wells:
The problem is that evangelical faith is accessible. The evangelistic appeal is necessary and clear but as soon as you move away from this appeal to something more nuanced and subtle, it gets too complicated. We don't know what we believe in anymore, and so anything other than the set positions is seen to be liberal.

Sam Wells:
The rhetoric surrounding these issues, particularly the gay issue, hides a deep fear. If you challenge people and ask; 'Is homosexual physical practice on the brink of destroying the whole universe?' The rational answer you eventually get is: 'Well, not really.' So I want to know why this conversation is discussed in such an intense and tortured way.

These same people often think: 'Well, if you can't trust the Bible on this, then the whole thing, the whole Bible falls.' There's always that sense of being on the edge of the abyss and that's the anxiety.

The problem is, you're never actually on the issue that really counts. I presume the issue that really counts is trusting the Bible when it says: 'God was in Christ reconciling the world to Himself.' That's the piece, the blade of grass that's closest to the edge of the cliff, I assume. Yet I don't think I've ever been in a room where someone's actually said that. Hundreds of blades of grass back from the edge of the cliff is Leviticus' teaching on sexuality, but that blade of grass is fought over with the intensity as if it was the last one.

Stanley Hauerwas:
One of the things I recommend is to not use the language of 'ethics'. I think it gives you an idea that you know what you're talking about and the sense that you're dealing with a specifi-

able area that's distinguished from etiquette. Part of what you're saying about the problems of evangelical life is related to the fact that the language we're using isn't doing any work. The problem about homosexuality, it seems to me, is not homosexuality, it's that we don't know what we're doing when we get married, and so, we don't know what marriage is.

So I wouldn't talk about homosexuality. I'd start by trying to ask: 'what kind of formation do we need to help the community figure out what conditions people need to be happily married?' To get at the issue, before we talk about homosexuality, we could talk about promiscuity. I mean that would be an interesting deal, but most people don't want to talk about promiscuity. We all know that the sexual wilderness in which we live seizes our imaginations in ways that are very hard to discipline. So, before you talk about homosexuality, say: 'How can we start thinking about what it means to not think about sex all the time because we've got other interesting things to do?'

Part of what my work represents is the attempt to change the subject by reframing issues. You have to find where people's challenges are and how the language will do work. The reason that so many people are so sure there's got to be something wrong with homosexuality is because they don't know why they do or don't have sex before marriage. They don't know why they only have sex with the people they are married to, they don't know what happens when they divorce and remarry, and what that means; they don't know any of that, they don't have a deep sense of what any of these terms mean any more or how to practice them faithfully. So what they cling to instead is a sense that homosexuality must be wrong.

Now, exactly how do we help recover a sense of how language can do real work. You don't become patient, you don't teach someone how to become patient by saying:

'You know, you really need to work to develop the habit of patience.' How on earth would you do that? The way you become patient is by, for example, undergoing all the discipline necessary to learn to draw or something like that. *The virtues ride on the back of good activity; you don't get them directly.* So you've got to find the activity that becomes constitutive of a way of life.

Luke Bretherton:
A positive take on what you are saying Stanley is this: people feel under pressure; they know that when they go to large shopping centres they feel comfortable and that it feels OK. Then they go to church and sit slightly bored in a not very well prepared sermon and that doesn't feel OK. But they also have a sense of the truth they are being told in church, the truth that tells them: 'There is a better story of the world here, there is a better story to live by.' But there is a chasm and they wonder: 'How do I form a life against these huge, very seductive forces in which I'm immersed, forces that stop me living out this better story? Maybe somehow, if I can get some positions, get some stakes in the ground, that'll give me something to hold onto in the tornado.'

Steve Chalke:
Yeah, stakes in the road to protect us from the slippery slope of theological and moral suicide.

I do some work for a big Christian conference in the UK called Spring Harvest. Spring Harvest is delivered by a staff team, but the topics are developed by the theme group. Russ and I are both on it. It's a small group that comes up with the concept, curriculum, and theme for each year's event. About three or four years ago, as part of my role on the group, I came up with a number of core themes for the development of Spring Harvest over the years ahead which were a bit edgy. I was already viewed by some evangelicals as slightly dangerous because of my published views on what is known as 'penal substitution' as a way of understanding the cross. In the end, I became aware that a number of Spring Harvest staff members were fearful that, because of the kind of questions that our curriculum was raising, the theme group was leading them all over the edge of a theological cliff. For instance, once you start asking questions about nuancing a view around homosexuality, everybody's scared about where it's going and where it's going to end. Are we all headed down the slippery slope to abandoning the Bible and its authority? That becomes the fear.

Jo Bailey Wells:
But for evangelicals, in their terms, history bears out the slippery slope story over and over again. It's the story of all these Christian institutions that are founded as good colleges where people promise not to drink and not to smoke  and not to dance. The institutions gradually lift all the stipulations and they turn into liberal elite institutions that are suspicious of Christians.

Luke Bretherton:
I didn't finish what the problem was exactly. You see, you have these stakes in the ground which you can hold on to against the tornado of the culture, or liberalism, or secular humanism, or however you frame the bug bear. But the point is, the culture has formed you in such a way that you don't do the hard work necessary of laying bricks or learning to lay bricks, learning to draw, or learning the disciplines of careful listening and reading your Bible daily, or regular prayer, or the kinds of things that would form you to allow you to make the appropriate judgements about what is faithful and what it unfaithful in a changing environment. So the stakes become a kind of procedural replacement for practices and habits that form you in ways that genuinely allow you to live a faithful life. The more you threaten the stakes, the more shrill the response. 'If you take the stakes out, I'm going over the edge of the cliff, I'm

going down the slippery slope.' The difficulty is how to get people to unclasp the stakes they are holding on to and begin to immerse themselves in practices that form them faithfully.

Stanley Hauerwas:
OK. Well I think what is killing evangelicalism is money, and money is just a name for greed. It's very interesting: most people are ready to talk about lust because they think they know what it looks like. Think how seldom they talk about greed because they don't know what it looks like. This is what greed looks like: 'I just had to have it for security.' It's an individualism that's underwritten by money, an individualism that says, 'I don't need anyone else; I can save myself.'

For evangelicalism to survive, it has to put people at risk to need one another, to make them vulnerable. That means they've got to risk their children. But to survive, we need to want to produce people that are as dysfunctional as the world in which we find ourselves. People have to give their children to that process as well. They've got to be willing to let them engage in the kind of work that doesn't look like it's going to be safe. This is just a kind of bottom line for reclaiming basic habits of vulnerability through which we discover our need for one another. Evangelicalism puts far too much emphasis upon belief rather than creating communities of vulnerability.

Steve Chalke:
I was interested in what Stanley was saying about money being the hedge that we need in an individualistic world. It buys us the autonomy and the security we need.

Sam Wells:
OK, going back to Stanley's phrase about doing work, I think if we continue with money, the question is; 'Is money being asked to do the work that money can do to form community?' One of the ways that this happens in self-styled 'growing churches' is the building campaign. The way we all talk about this is: 'This building campaign is just two years of pain we have to endure to raise the money to build an extra sanctuary or whatever it might be.' But, in fact, the campaign itself is

more important than the future sanctuary because people are parting with money for a shared project and are becoming economically interdependent. In other words, they are actu-ally forming a community and *money is actually working to create interdependence rather than lapsing into being a form of personal security.*

It's not that money doesn't have a role to play in church. It's that we have to receive it as a gift for making us dependent on one another and dependent on God. The most impressive times happen when you call for that second collection. People do give sacrificially and then the money actually does some community-forming work.

Stanley's question would be then, what kind of community do we need to be in order to trust in relationships more than we trust in money to get us out of trouble. That's the virtue question. Additionally, what kinds of communal projects make us believe that actually more security lies in the project than in our health insurance or the other reasons we might need money. Part of the problem is we find it very difficult to articulate what these projects might be. We can talk about world peace and the need to end poverty now and these kinds of things, but these are just abstract terms.

Shane Claiborne:
It seems that that's why the church really thrives in crisis, in persecution and struggle. You have to have community. So, there's a terrible storm in New Orleans and congregations and communities just come together. They understand that they need each other. There is no delusion or fantasy of independence that says: 'I don't need other people.' It's about the nature of the kingdom of God and we don't have rich folks and poor folks. We just have family and that's going to affect the way

that you look at your possessions, you know, and look at your home, and look at your money.

Luke Bretherton:
But I think it goes back to what Stanley was saying before, about how to produce people who don't fit with the aspirations of our culture; people who don't fit the dominant criteria of success that are laid out. Another name for money is 'aspiration', the western dream, and it's a big problem in churches. You'll live in a better house than your parents, your kids will go to college and they'll get a better job than you. That trajectory of aspiration becomes the dominant story and often people aren't even aware that it is that story, the story of the Western dream, that they are living by.

In the churches in London that I'm involved in, there's a mentality of 'get in, get up, get out.' People think of the city as just 'an instrument for my advancement'. 'I go to this church because it gives me some friends to cope with the pressures of living on this trajectory of aspiration. As nice as my friends are, there will reach a point where I'll no longer need them.' Often what then happens is people who function with this mentality will get out of the city. They'll get to a nicer, quieter place and their kids will go to a good school. They will stop going to church because now that they've got the security of money, they no longer need the security of friends. Whereas the Diaspora chur-ches—whether it's the Brazil-ian Pentecostal churches or whatever—their members are very aware that

they need friends because no one's got any money. They have very large churches; the friends are the substitute for the money. For them church is the place where you are put in touch with people who can help you.

I think the challenge is how to question how your life dream orientates you to money: is money something you use for the common good? Or is it a straightjacket that stops you reaching out to others? These kinds of question really deal with the issue of envisioning a kind of Christian life that is more compelling and more inspirational than the Western dream. Shane, I'd be interested to know about the kind of young people who come to do work with you. What are their passions? Do you think that they're trying to hook into a different vision of life and a different future, a different life dream as it were?

Shane Claiborne:
Yeah, I think there is a different aspiration among them. I can remember one young woman who was talking to Tony Campolo at Eastern University. She explained that she applied to one of the most prestigious suburban schools to teach. Out of 300 applicants, she got this job. Tony just asked: 'Why in the world would you settle for that job? There are 299 other people waiting in line to take the job. You're one of the best teachers that we have coming out of this school. You should be going to some of the toughest schools in the city.'

I think that's the paradigm shift. Young people are not just asking themselves: 'Am I going to be a doctor, lawyer, or teacher?' but '*What kind of* doctor, lawyer, or teacher am I going to be?' It's a new way of thinking about who I am—not just what I'm going to do, but who I'm becoming. I see that everywhere.

I met a kid who was a robotics engineer who said: 'I used to be doing this just because I could make a lot of money or do something to impress people. Now I'm starting to ask myself why I've been given these gifts.' He had gotten a group of robotics engineers together and they began working to design robots that dismantle land mines. They wanted to send them over to Afghanistan so that the robots could disarm field mines, a job that currently blows off little kids' fingers.

These kinds of aspirations only come from a renewed imagination, the sense of not conforming to the patterns of the world but being transformed by the renewing of our mind. We see this in Scripture too. Zacchaeus and Matthew and these tax collectors are totally transformed. Some of them stay tax collectors, but they all stop conforming to the system of the world that they live in. Non-conformity doesn't mean uniformity. Non-conformity doesn't mean we all respond exactly the same way, although we certainly are being transformed into a new creation.

Sam Wells:
This issue of non-conformity is really interesting. Thinking of the church as a whole, I wonder if we are just pushovers, not really non-conformists. We don't have a sense of crisis, a real understanding of what it means to be in the world but not of the world. In that sense, Stanley's complaint is the same as Karl Barth's in 1914. When it really comes to a crunch, we are pushovers. We have no backbone to stand up against the dissolution of the kingdom of God. If we understand Satan's work to be some kind of power that's taking over the world one community at a time, and 'breaking the will' of each community by torturing the leaders, would we be among the pushovers or among the tortured? Considering the state of the church right now: we would probably just join the other side. It's comfortable there; they have jobs and so on.

If we're going to be a community that's worth torturing, that actually constitutes a threat, we can't be wasting time on the kind of things that dissolve our backbone from the inside. We have to be a disciplined, tight-knit community. We have to keep our promises to one another. We have to be able to trust one another because we are the underground. And the problem for Barth in 1914 was that all these professors just put their hands up and said: 'OK, we'll go with the Kaiser.' They were pushovers and their actions discredited everything they had said up to that point. Their life's work suddenly didn't amount to anything.

So the question for us right now is: 'What do we finally stand for? Are we a colony of the kingdom of God, or are we a bunch of individual people arranging our own salvation as if it were our retirement plan, securing our own selves?' St Paul suggests we are to be most pitied if *that's* what we're about, if we're just about securing our own futures. The kingdom is discovered by people who have made strong commitments to one another. They know they can't do it on their own.

It's all about how we can make ourselves and allow ourselves to be made into that kind of counter-community. The disciples couldn't afford to be wasting time with their own individual proclivities; they just couldn't afford that distraction. This had to be a tight knit group because they had important things to do.

This all goes back to an idea of narrative and purpose. The evangelical community in England, as well as many others, has not been good enough at articulating what worthwhile projects might unite us. As we think about what these projects might be, we have to realise that what's good for the church may not be identical to the nation's projects. Popular or not, we need to do what's good *for the church.*

Luke Bretherton:

That raises the question about the anxiety about the slippery slope and the fear of giving up on positional morality. It seems that you're giving up on discipline, but actually, the issue is not on giving up discipline or even on law. Rather, we're hung up on *wrong* laws—we've misunderstood the laws and we are completely ill-disciplined. *If we are stuck in a positional morality, then we are not on a slippery slope but way downstream and being washed out to sea.* What we really need to do is re-understand genuine discipline.

Sam Wells:

This relates to a point that Stanley makes about atonement theories. The problem, not just with substitutionary atonement theories, but actually with all the conventional terms and theories, is that they are a way of by-passing the church. They don't need us to be a restored community. You might even say that they are a way of by-passing Israel. They are all a way of giving Christians salvation without Israel, without the community, without the people of God.

The same is true for these laws, these stakes in the ground. If you keep your nose clean, you actually don't need each other. You don't need the church. It's Gnosticism, a kind of personal, individual escape rapture where God plucks you out of the morass. That's the problem at the heart of it—that you can just do it by yourself. By contrast, to be virtuous you need other people to help form you.

Steve Chalke:
If all that's true, in your definition, is there a difference between laws and rules? Are there *any* stakes in the ground? You know, last night I mentioned Bonhoeffer and the attempt to kill Hitler. You both seemed to say very quickly: 'Thou shalt not kill.' So it struck me: 'There's a stake.' So who decides what stakes remain in the ground after the rest have been cleared away?

Sam Wells:
Virtue ethics puts *habits* in the place where *commands* used to be. Let's take marriage for example. Rather than saying 'Do not commit adultery', it says 'eat together every evening.' With eating together every evening, somebody has to go shopping, somebody has to prepare the food, somebody has to clear up afterwards, somebody has to say every single time: 'Should we put some flowers on the table?' When the phone rings: 'Shall we answer it?' Every single gesture is actually building up a marriage or reducing it. Every single time you must decide to arrange food on the plate or to dump it down in front of your partner. All of those things can be done with care and love, they can be done punctually or they can be done aggressively. If you get eating together in the evening right, you've got a marriage. Even if you don't commit adultery, there are a hundred other ways to destroy a marriage. You might not even notice that your marriage is falling apart because, you think: 'We kept the rule so it's not our fault, I haven't chased after anybody.' Living virtuously becomes about developing a habit, in this case, what it means to eat together every evening. Out of this habit grow other questions about the way to live: 'Should it be just the two of us? Should there be children here?

Should there be neighbours here? When people just drop in, do we say to them: "This is our evening to be together", or do we say, "Come on in"?' You put the emphasis on eating together well and then you realise that the night before he died Jesus said to his disciples: "Let's eat together."

Russell Rook:
In that case, to push these questions further, do the rules decide the habits or the habits decide the rules? Do you start with 'Do not commit adultery' and that leads you to say: 'If I'm not going to commit adultery, what kind of habits do I need to develop?'

Sam Wells:
Yeah, it's difficult to imagine how you could have the meal together if certain things were or weren't happening. That's why Stanley talks about sacraments. If eating together is at the heart of the Church, then you need to ask questions like: 'Who needs to be there?' So you do evangelism to bring these kinds of people  to the meal so that it's actually a proper meal. Your relationship with the Jews is not because you regret the holocaust. It's because you can't understand the Eucharist unless you're in conversation with Jews about the Passover.

As for the rules, it's not like rules aren't important. Rules are important in communicating a whole tradition and a whole narrative and a whole history to people in a manageable two sentence phrase. Rules are very helpful for new comers; they're very helpful for outsiders; they're very helpful for a little reminder if we get confused, but they don't do the work on their own. You have to inhabit rules with a whole history. In the end, it's those meals you've had together over twenty five years that constitute your marriage rather than who you didn't sleep with.

Put it this way: The Ten Commandments are Exodus chapter 20, they're not Exodus chapter 1. You can only read the Ten Commandments if you read the first nineteen chapters and you read the rest of Exodus afterwards. There is no such thing as a de-contextualized rule; *all rules are immersed in a narrative.* The Bible gives us the Christian story in narratives through which rules have emerged. The desire to pluck ten sentences out of the Bible and say: 'This is it', is a mistake. You can only understand the Ten Commandments if you realise that they are a covenant that has emerged after lib-eration. If you try to understand liberation without covenant, you are making an even bigger mistake than trying to understand covenant without liberation. They're all wrapped up with each other.

Stanley Hauerwas:
They are not isolated from one another. When I used to teach the core course in Christian ethics, I would start the course by saying: 'If you need this course in order to know how to live a well lived life, it's too late. You're already too corrupt to understand what I'm going to do. But if you need a short hand, I'm going to tell you right now in a second what you need to be able to survive the ministry with integrity—Don't lie! Don't lie. Write it down. That's enough.'

Luke Bretherton:
Very short course!

Stanley Hauerwas:
Don't lie. Now think about that. Think about how that pulls you into other questions: 'What kind of economic relations do I need to have so that I don't lie?' 'How do I understand the way I relate to other people outside my marriage, that I don't lie to my spouse?' 'How do I avoid self-deception?' If I don't acknowledge God and God's history among the chosen people, I ignore something that's actually constitutive of telling the truth about the way the world is.

So, how is all of this interrelated? Does it allow me to discover that my life is located intelligibly within that story? If I'm not able to think that way, then I have to ask myself: 'What stories am I living out that I may not know how to acknowledge?' That's what it means to be gripped by a power—being gripped by a power means living out a story that you do not have the ability to acknowledge. There's no way you're going to discover that on your own. You will only discover it if you have a friend who loves you enough to tell you, and most of the time we don't want our friends to hurt us.

Shane Claiborne:
A couple of thoughts: Dorothy Day said our work is to create a society where it's easier to be good. That doesn't just happen magically. For us, community is a place where we've got to be really *deliberate*. A lot of our rules come from trying to figure out how to be a deliberate community. For example, we don't have alcohol in our houses—not because we think it's a terrible sin to grab a beer, but because we're trying to make a safe place for the folks that are most vulnerable. Many of my housemates have struggled with addiction and things like that. Sometimes they have been really formed around that addiction and we have to unashamedly decode that.

I read a great article in a journal on parenting where someone was interviewing one of the hands-off parenting gurus. He was one of those social psychologists that said, 'Let kids touch the stove and learn what hot is, let them make mistakes and learn.' The interviewer asked the social psychologist, 'What did you learn?' He replied, 'It all looked good on paper, but really we've created a generation of brats.'

In a lot of ways we are in danger of creating a generation of spiritual brats, who react to the legalism that we grew up with. 'Don't smoke, don't drink', all that. Now these kids are saying, 'We're not going to tell anybody how to live.' This mentality doesn't move us closer to the environment where it's easier to be good. Years into our communal life, we had to begin to really ask: 'What beliefs and

practices are non-negotiable?' 'What stakes will we put in the ground?' We have a statement of our core beliefs and our core practices that foster discipline in our community. If you think about it, 'disciple' and 'discipline' share the same linguistic root. We have to work out our salvation, and a community creates a critical mass moving towards that goal of salvation together.

A lot of times I say that community is about surrounding ourselves with people who look like the person we want to become. We see Jesus in those people and by sharing our lives with them they move us closer to being like Jesus. For example, I saw one of my college buddies who took off his own boots when he passed a homeless guy on the street. Then he put the homeless man's shoes on his own feet. I thought to myself: 'Man! That looks like Jesus!' Those kinds of people continue to push us closer to who we want to be.

Stanley Hauerwas:
I don't think you ever want to make discipline *an end in itself.* Discipline comes because you want to learn how to dribble a basketball. You don't realise it's discipline when you're doing it; you just want to learn how to dribble the ball. It's hard work to do it over and over and over again, but it's part of a practice you find so enthralling that you don't realise it's discipline.

Luke Bretherton:
Using your basketball analogy, 'saint' is a name that Christians give to really good 'basketball' players. That's where using your point about friends becomes important; you require people who challenge you, people who hold you accountable and push you further. The story of the Church consists of all these stories, whether it's Francis of Assisi or local saints who exemplify what it means to practice really thoroughly over years and years. It's really important to name those examples that really live out the virtuous life, people who practice hard and are true to this stuff.

Russell Rook:
People like that don't start with discipline in mind. Instead, they start with the end in sight. So, the desire to be like Jesus means repeatedly performing these really small actions.

There's a story about Picasso. I don't know if it's true, but it's a really great story. When he was young someone told him that it was impossible to draw a perfect circle. So Picasso spent pretty much the whole of this life trying to prove them wrong. And by the end of his life, he  had mastered the technique and could draw one perfect circle free hand.

How many times did he have to try to do it, until he got to that point where he could do it? How much practice did it take him to perform what was seemingly impossible? Well, I want to be like Jesus. I know it feels impossible, but if I take my shoes off and swap them with the homeless guy, and if I do this and I practice these habits, then actually, there is this possibility that I can become like him.

Shane Claiborne:
It's not just about bad people becoming good but about dead people coming to life. Taking your example Sam, it's not just the morality of keeping the law about adultery. Even if the couple did manage to keep the law, if they weren't alive they weren't bringing other people to life. The disciplines have been about *life*. For me, getting rid of television wasn't fun at first, I felt a little withdrawal. Or going for a jog five miles, I didn't like that at first but then I felt myself breathing better. When our community got rid of the TV, there was a period of withdrawal, but then we started to feel ourselves come to life. We live by laws because Jesus wants to bring us in closer to him, the Spirit is pointing us towards life to the fullest. Laws are not just guilt or an obligation.

Stanley Hauerwas:
Here's another way to talk about laws, especially about Leviticus. Leviticus still poses a deep challenge to us: just think about the price Israel had to pay. Leviticus is about a people

who are called by God to live in the world that doesn't want them. Israel needs this stuff, these laws, to be able to survive as a holy people in a world that doesn't want them. If you read it as if it's going to underwrite the way the world is, then it's just rubbish. But if you see Leviticus as a training manual for the army against armies, then it looks pretty interesting.

Russell Rook:
Are we saying that the real core of the matter in Exodus and Leviticus is a vision for God's people, a narrative for them to live up to? Christian ethics should be a pre-eminent *vision*; an aspiration to really be God's people? The actual laws, be they the Ten Com-mandments or some of the particular laws in Leviticus, kind of mark the parameters of that vision. They protect that vision.

Increasingly, rather than proclaim the vision, the church just polices the parameters. Instead, we should proclaim: 'This is what it means to be God's people.' To use some of our examples, being God's people means sitting down with your wife every evening and having a meal with your kids. It's practicing habits. It's not about not getting divorced, not being homosexual, not doing this, not having bad thoughts, not watching the wrong TV programs.

Jo Bailey Wells:
Can I put that a different way around? The chorus of Leviticus, the reoccurring central idea: 'Be holy as I am holy,' is God inviting his   people to participate in his character and be like Him, whereas holiness in our common language has become a sort of distancing, holier than thou, competitive, one-upmanship—not attractive in the least. Holiness has lost its theological character; it's lost the fact that this is an invitation to be . . .

Shane Claiborne:
Set apart

Jo Bailey Wells:
Even the words 'set apart' don't make me terribly comfortable in that context. That tends to be the casual answer people give for the meaning of holiness. Holiness is just *who God is*. If there's one word to describe God, it's holy, but the concept has lost its attractive, magnetic, invitational force.

Steve Chalke:
In our Spring Harvest theme group, we started talking around what compromises God's nature or character. The group started talking about his justice, his mercy, his compassion, his judgement, etc. In this context someone referred to his holiness. But holiness is not so much a character trait as an umbrella term—an overarching statement that sums up God's whole character and the contents of it. If the question is: 'What is God's holiness?' the answer is: His holiness is all of his character traits put together—justice, mercy, compassion, etc. And, as you go through this exercise you end up with a great definition of how to live.

Shane Claiborne:
We need to remember the idea of God forming a contrast society, a contrast culture, when we read the Law. It's not simply a counter-culture reacting to the dominant culture. We are forming a new culture. For our biblical ancestors, the Law set them apart from the world they came from; they had peculiar ways of living, eating, and dressing. God was saying: 'If you don't do these things, you're going to end up like Egypt again.' God hates sin, hates the breaking of the Law *because it destroys us*. Being like Egypt destroys us and God can't stand to watch us hurt ourselves.

In the church today, the only reason God's 'cultural refugees' seem so peculiar is because of how far the world has moved from God's dream for it. We should live in ways that don't make sense without God. God's people look strange in a rebellious and fallen world.

Luke Bretherton:
Leviticus is only a part of a whole story about how to form a people who can be holy like God is holy. The laws do not arrive like a computer program delivered over the internet. It's an interactive process and Leviticus is the testimony of a people's dialogue with God. Their wrestling with God, like Jacob, forges a form of life that can sustain what it might mean to live up to that distinction, the command: 'Be holy as I am holy.' This chorus in Leviticus is a promise and an invitation.
Jo Bailey Wells:
And a *demand*: A promise, an invitation, and a demand.

Endnotes

[1] Edited from a conversation recorded at Duke Divinity School, Durham, NC, USA, 13th August, 2009.

Chapter 2

Theology as Narrative

Samuel Wells

Three strands

There are three broad strands in contemporary writing on Christian ethics. One we might call 'universal'. The universal approach is principally concerned with finding common ground. Its focus is questions and dilemmas in the public sphere. These include the beginning and end of life, the beginning and conduct of war, the appropriate balance between nature and technology, and issues of global concern such as climate change and the distribution of wealth. It is not generally innovative methodologically. It is usually happy to work with the conventional deontological and consequential categories in seeking to find common cause with nonreligious approaches for the treatment and resolution of issues of public concern. As far as it seeks to articulate a specific Christian contribution to these debates, it is generally guided by the modern need to make Christianity reasonable and useful, as a discipline that seeks understanding that suits all people in all situations. This might be termed 'ethics for anybody'.[1]

A second strand we might call 'subversive'. The subversive approaches begin in an attitude of rebellion. On closer inspection, the rebellion is perhaps not so much against the idea that there can be a universal ethic; the point at issue is that the universal ethic tends to be dictated by the powerful, and thus is not truly universal at all, but just a minority view spoken with a loud and influential voice. Beneath this loud and influential voice lies a thread of violence. Such violence is plausible because if a view truly is universal, dissent may quickly seem irrational and reprehensible, and in need of swift correction. Subversive ethics protests at the way the 'mainstream' account suppresses alternative voices, excluded for reasons of gender, race, or other social or environmental location, and seeks to make those voices heard, thereby questioning the apparent consensus.

The positive agenda that follows from making these voices heard is more diverse. (One is conscious of Kin Hubbard's observation. 'It's going to be fun to watch and see how long the meek can keep the earth after they inherit it.') Some see the church as a way of restoring an inclusive society where no voices are suppressed. This is the more optimistic view. Such people sometimes look to recover and attend to neglected parts of church history. They may for example find periods or places where women's ministry was accepted and valued, where different races were harmoniously incorporated into one fellowship, or where a healthy relationship between human beings and the rest of creation flourished. Others conclude less hopefully that the church will always be wedded to the powerful, that there will never be an inclusive society, and that faithfulness lies in appealing to a new quasi-church of marginalized values. This might be called 'ethics for the excluded.'[2]

A third strand, which we might call 'ecclesial', seeks to articulate a distinctive theological ethic. This theological ethic has significant similarities and differences with the previous two approaches. It seeks dialogue with other traditions, but not in the way the 'universal' approach does. It perceives that the universal approach does less than justice to the particularity of the Christian tradition. Ecclesial ethics is concerned with the liberating power of Christianity, but not quite in the way the 'subversive' approach is. It considers that liberation lies in identifying the particularity of the tradition, rather than in overcoming or ignoring it. It also assumes that if the church is to be faithful, it must always be the church of the poor. The much-quoted saying 'The poor are always with you' means not '. . .

and therefore you can ignore them,' but '. . . and therefore you are always with the poor.' The subversive approach is stronger on particularity than the universal strand, but has an anthropology that the ecclesial approach sees as still too much wedded to individual autonomy or self-expression. Ecclesial ethics considers that liberation lies not specifically with the articulation and expression of experience but with the traditions and practices of the church and the character and acts of God. This might be called 'ethics for the church.' This study pursues this third approach.

At this stage I am concerned to point out that each kind of ethics—universal, subversive, and ecclesial—presupposes a story. I shall now outline what that claim means.

Underlying narratives in Christian ethics

The story presupposed by the universal approach is the most difficult to identify, because it is the least self-conscious. But that makes its identification and description all the more important. It is difficult to identify because what I am calling the universal approach covers a considerable variety of methods, each with its own first principles. The proponents of these methods have tended to be rather more conscious of the ways in which their methods differed from other methods than they have of the ways in which all of the methods made common assumptions. Indeed, it is perhaps only when the voices of those who have experience being excluded from the story have made themselves heard that universal ethics has begun to appear as a story at all, and not simply a right and natural order inhabited by competing perceptions.

The simplest way to explore some of these methods is to notice the elements of the Christian faith each method takes to be foundational. A variety of models present themselves, of which five may be mentioned here. One model of theology takes its notion of theology to begin with reflection on and study of sacred *texts*—notably, the books of the Bible. These texts are taken to be distillations of wisdom beyond that reachable by unaided human reflection. They are considered,

together and separately, as revelation. The purpose of theology
is to provide an exegesis of these sacred texts. Another model
of theology is to locate the foundational substance behind the
texts in the *events* the texts describe. This approach sees sacred
events as central, and the texts as one means, perhaps the best
but certainly not the only, of getting to the sacred events.
Theology is principally concerned with establishing the history
of these vital events. A third model of theology sees truth as
lying beyond texts and even events, and instead in a logical
system of interlocking *doctrines* describing the person and
activity of the sacred being, God. Dogmatic inquiry and reflection thus exist to distill ordered and plausible truth from a
range of sources, including text, event, and practice. Sometimes
non-theological discourse is given a higher status in this
inquiry, and the object is to produce a *philosophical* system
rather than a dogmatic one.

With the turn to the subject associated with the
Enlightenment, it has become more common for theology to be
considered as the study of sacred *experience*—not necessarily of
sacred characters long ago, but particularly of the range of
experience accessible to the contemporary heart and mind.
And this is the point at which the narrative character of the
universal approach begins to emerge. For it quickly appears
that some people's experience seems to count for more than
others'. If an experience is related that questions, challenges, or
contradicts the accepted wisdom, it can be very difficult for
that experience to get a hearing. What is revealed is the social
structure of knowledge. A whole series of implicit power relations emerges. There are unspoken rules governing who gets
to decide if something is legitimate, valuable, or true. And this
discovery is where subversive ethics begins.

Subversive ethics constantly highlights the power relations
at work in theological and other discourse. The winners have
written not just the history, but the theology too. So, to take the
most common example, men have constructed a theology of a
male God: this has underwritten a patriarchal social structure
and inhibited women's freedom, experience, voices, ministries, lives.[3] To take a similarly oft-quoted example, the intimate link between Christianity, commerce, and 'civilization' in

the scramble for Africa contrived, in many cases, to leave faith in the hearts of the conquered and land in the hands of the conqueror.[4] In another sphere, reflection on the experience of faith among the poorest residents of Latin American countries has enabled many to articulate that their principal encounter with God takes place not in the pietist quietism commended by some of their church leaders but in the active attempt to take control of their own economic and social destiny.[5] Again, a suitable reading of the creation story has given permission to an ideology of domination over the nonhuman creation that has left the two-thirds world and its rain forests and marginal lands reeling from the rampaging demands of the rich countries' consumers.[6]

In each case the widespread experience of the 'excluded' has been that their experience seems to be part of a different story from the prevailing theological and social narrative. The rival notions of theology as exegesis of sacred texts, history of sacred events, formation of a dogmatic or philosophical system, or reflection on sacred experience seem, in the light of these rival and excluded stories, to have rather more significant agreements than differences. Universal ethics presupposes that there is one story, but masks that story in the assumption that it is everybody's story. Subversive ethics, by beginning with the experience of exclusion and oppression, points out that this (by no means universal) ideology has an implicit story; that this story is an instrument of domination; and that in fact there are numerous rival stories, representing a host of suppressed parties. Sometimes subversive ethics can take a 'modern' turn and substitute a new metanarrative for the one it has supplanted—assuming, for example, that Marx's story of class struggle defines the Latin American context. More often, subversive ethics takes a postmodern turn and rejoices in the many liberated narratives and previously forgotten histories, whether they are compatible with one another or not. The notion of coherence can become secondary to the emphasis on the authentic and legitimate voicing of the experience of oppression.

This therefore is the perception of many in the theological world: that the denial of narrative and the emphasis on propo-

sitional truth is an acquiescence in a oppressive system of
power relations; that any form of overarching metanarrative is
likely to be a covert form of oppression by other means; and
that the discovery, permission, and affirmation of previously
suppressed stories is an imperative that supersedes that quest
for a single, coherent expression of truth. What therefore might
it mean to talk of narrative in ecclesial terms?

Ecclesial ethics and its discontents

Ecclesial ethics is ethics *for the church*. Each of the previous definitions of theology had an understanding of the location of the
discipline. Some saw that location in a particularly text; some in
a particular sequence of events, described by the text; some in
a particular order of doctrinal or philosophical thought. A
counterview saw theology residing in human experience, particularly in the experience of oppression and exclusion.
Ecclesial ethics has its own definition of theology. It sees the key
location of theology as being in the practices of the church. This
is only secondarily about a sacred text, sequence of events, or
set of doctrines; it is primarily about the formation, development, and renewal of a sacred *people*. It is this people, the sacred
community, that is the center of ethical reflection. This is what
God wants as his witness in his world and as companion in the
kingdom. This is what Jesus came into the world to embody
and gave his life to make possible. This is what the Bible was
written to encourage and guide, and this is what theologians
are called to resource and challenge. The sacred community is
the touchstone of virtue. That which builds it up and enables it
to be faithful is good and right and true; that which attempts to
bypass it or contrives to render it invisible or undermines it
from within is dubious, misguided, or dangerous.

The story presupposed by ecclesial ethics is as follows:
Israel was called to be a priestly kingdom and a holy nation.
Being holy meant being distinctive and being like God. Being
priestly meant that other nations would benefit from the 'ministry' of Israel so long as Israel retained its distinctiveness. God
then gave Israel everything it needed to be holy and priestly. It

had the Law to guarantee God's promise and reveal God's heart. It had the land in which to grow and flourish. It had, in due time, a king to provide unity under God and leadership in God's ways. And it had the temple to enshrine its covenant with God and to restore that relationship whenever the people went astray. Land, king, and temple were lost in the exile, and each was restored only in parody. Though the people returned to the Lord, they were ruled by foreigners. Though there were sometimes kings, there was no return to the tradition of David. Though there was a new temple, there was no ark of the covenant at the heart of it. But during the exile the people's sense of what constituted the covenant was renewed, and this renewal provided the space in which God did a new thing for and with his people.

Jesus embodied that renewed covenant and redefined land, king, and temple. He called to him a renewed people, with continuities going back before the exile (twelve apostles representing the twelve tribes) but also with resonances of a people returning from exile (the incorporation of outcasts, the unclean, tax collectors, and women). He directed the people's attention to an eschatological horizon beyond the land dominated by the Romans. He pointed out that the second temple had not brought reconciliation with God and spoke of his body as a new temple. The resultant conflict was played out on his body, in his passion and death. Through his resurrection and the sending of the Spirit, his disciples realized that a new and definitive reconciliation had taken place. Meanwhile, the notion of his 'body' had changed. Now it was they who, in the practices of forming their common life—incorporating newcomers, maintaining the community, deliberating over its good order, and restoring it when it faced the setbacks of external persecution and internal dissent or weakness—it was they who, in these practices, were now his body. They were a royal priesthood and a holy nation. They had a vocation to imitate God in Christ and to offer their distinctive life as a gift to the world. And they, too, found that God gave them everything they needed to follow him. Paul's journey to Rome echoed Jesus' journey to Jerusalem. As Jesus' journey focused the hopes of Israel, so Paul's journey opened those hopes out to the whole world.

The centuries that followed brought periodic persecution, and this, together with the desire to incorporate the maximum number of newcomers into its fellowship, made the offer of increasing involvement in the government of the empire from the early fourth century very attractive. However, the price of this was to make the church largely invisible. The journey to 'universal' ethics names these ways in which the church became invisible. The location of theology and ethics ceased to be the sacred community, the holy people, and became a host of other things. The journey of St Antony symbolizes this change.[7] The conversion of the Roman emperor meant that one battle had been won, but another had been lost. Antony left Alexandria, the great city of antique culture, to set up his cell in the Egyptian desert as the first of the Desert Fathers. The battleground was no longer on the boundary of church and world. It was now in the human heart, between flesh and spirit.

Three temptations have misled the church ever since the time of St Antony. The first is to see the principal location of theology as the world, or 'society'—the political whole. By making the church invisible this approach gives up on God's primary mode of working in the world. It also opens the church's heart to further temptations. Christians may begin to confuse the church and the world, trying to make the world the church, or treating it as if it were. If Christians do not have a distinctive community, they will seek prominent positions amongst the powerful in the world. They may well regard it as their responsibility, rather than God's, to make the world come out right, to usher in the kingdom. They will therefore need to form a different set of allies, and find themselves with a different set of enemies. This is the danger of 'universal' ethics. And this is before it even starts to coerce those who disagree.[8]

A second, contrasting, temptation often corresponds with a very negative, even dualist, view of the status of creation. The temptation is to assume that because the sacred community is the key location of theology, because God's principal way of working in the world is through the church, then God has no purpose for the rest of his creation. This is putting the holiness of the community prior to the holiness of God. The church may be the principle way in which God works in the world, but it is by no means the only one. The church needs to be alive to all the ways in which God works in the world, not to confine itself to just one, albeit the principal one. Sectarianism is usually regarded as one way in which the church makes a problem for the world. The nature of this alleged problem is twofold. The existence of groups who emphasize their separateness weakens liberal democracy and makes conflict more likely. In the particularly case of Christian separateness, the world is furthermore deprived of the (perhaps ambiguous) advantage of the church's ministry, and of a healthy place in the church's theological scheme. But this is to see the issue the wrong way around. Sectarianism, is not primarily a problem for the world, although it can present dilemmas for liberal democracies. Sectarianism is on the contrary, primarily a problem for the church. It is a problem because a church that is cutting itself off largely or entirely from its surrounding society is thereby depriving itself of many of the ways in which God's grace is made plain in the world through the Holy Spirit. God is still giving the church all it needs to follow him, but the church is denying itself access to many of these gifts. It is like the third slave who buries his talent in the hillside—and it can expect the same reward. This temptation is much discussed and feared by social commentators—but is in fact relatively rarely adopted. It remains a temptation nonetheless.[9]

A third, more subtle, temptation can thrive under the guise of either of the previous two. It is to perceive that in the knowledge of certain key pieces of information, not universally available, one has a unique power—power, for example, to be intimate with God and to live with him eternally. This perception of a secret knowledge is known as Gnosticism. The name 'Gnosticism' is a term associated with a heresy of the second century. But the Enlightenment's turn to the subject and the contemporary desire to secure individual security and fulfillment provide fertile soil for a looser use of the term 'Gnostic.' For the Gnostic, the spiritual quest is an inherently individual matter. The location of theology, if such a term can still be used, lies in the heart and mind of each discrete individual. Human community is secondary, and is valuable only to encourage, resource, or stimulate the individual experience. Other people are more likely to be an obstacle than to be a requirement of fulfillment. Gnosticism consistently bypasses the need for human community and establishes communion with God on grounds that do not require the conversations and compromises and habits of regular contact with other people.

Within the second, 'sectarian' temptation Gnosticism underwrites a sense of superiority over the faithless, perhaps evil, world. The church becomes a group of people who each have a special knowledge, or an access to a special experience, that the world cannot have. While contact with the world might extend the number of people who may discover that knowledge or experience, it carries the perpetual risk of sullying or diminishing the knowledge or experience by sharing it with those who would not respect it or even seek to undermine it. The first, 'universal' temptation is a more commonplace to find it. Gnosticism tends to exist as an emphasis on personal piety, perhaps together with an emphasis on doctrinal purity. Thus Christians may engage in the most damaging public practices which still assuming that thinking 'the right things' about salvation or having a 'close personal relationship' with God ensures that righteousness remains with them.

A church whose members believe that the true location of theology lies in their own private knowledge and experience is desperately vulnerable. It is defenseless against an ideology that calls them to corporate commitment and sacrifice. So long as that ideology makes no demands on their doctrinal purity or individual experience it can persuade Christians to perform ghastly injustices and cruelties without realizing their error.[10] Such tragedies have taken place countless times in recent decades, from Auschwitz to Kigali, from Santiago to the Pentagon. The individual simply is not strong enough to carry the full weight of theological liberation—to become the church. Gnosticism delivers the church into captivity—into exile. What is needed is an understanding of the church that is not so committed to the universal or the individual that the church becomes invisible, but is meanwhile not so committed to the visibility of the church that it seeks to make the world invisible (at least to the church). What is needed is for the church to be restored as the primary location of theological and ethical enquiry.

This then is the story that ecclesial ethics presupposes, the 'narrative' that lies behind narrative ethics; and these are the temptations the telling of this story is designed to avoid. Four elements coalesce to make this distinctive ecclesial ethic. The church, the sacred community, is understood as the focus of God's purposes for the world, the witness of his grace, and the earnest of the destiny he has prepared for all of creation—friendship with God. The unit of ethics is neither the universal world nor the isolated individual but the particular church. The *narrative* I have outlined above is the way the church remembers its identity, recognizing that the failures and blind alleys are as significant as the saintly lives and golden eras. This narrative paints tiny human lives, plans, and histories into the awesome canvas of God's everlasting providence. It slips earnest efforts and ignoble failures into the pocket of God's original creation and final fulfillment. It embraces the tyranny of the pointless present with the everlasting arms of sacred memory and saving hope. The Christian story places Christ at the center of meaning and delvers humanity from the agony of meaninglessness, transforming the unavoidable fate of our mortal folly into the glorious destiny of his unending joy. Confidence in this story gives the church the resources to engage with other and rival stories. The center of the church's life is the practices through which the church is formed, extended, and restored. Through reading Scripture, baptizing, sharing communion, seeking God's forgiveness, being reconciled with one another, interceding, making peace, the church incorporates its tradition and offers a priestly ministry to the world. The church constantly reflects on the way it performs these practices, seeking always to be shaped into the life of Christ by carrying them out faithfully. Narrative and practices form *witnesses*—disciples who embody the church's life in prayer and service. These witnesses are the church's truth claim—it has no purchase on truth that is detached from the transformation of lives and communities brought about by its narrative and practices. Individuals are not the location of theological reflection, but they can be the symbols and narrative and sacramental transformation. Their changed lives embody the hope of the community. They are the most visible face of the church, the most public ambassadors of God.

Saints and heroes

A number of questions may still remain. How do these ecclesial witnesses differ from Gnostic individuals? How does the particularly of the church's narrative issue in lives of witness? What criteria define the faithfulness of that witness? Is Christianity about great individuals or about good communities? The answer to these questions lies in a significant distinction that summarizes the argument of this chapter. The distinction lies in a subtle difference between antique and theological wisdom.

Aristotle sought to inspire his readers to be heroes. The virtues he commends are noble ones, and the lives he advocates are ones of effort and attention. His followers will, if faithful, be capable of making decisive interventions that swing the course of a battle, or a debate, or a long cultural struggle. Without them, all might be lost. They are formed in the virtues required to negotiate an awesome role: they are prepared to be the center of the story. They stand out from the crowd; they form friendships only with others of similar stature. They are self-sufficient and resilient amid setbacks. The definitive icon of virtue is the soldier, who is prepared to risk death for the sake of a higher good. The noblest death is death in battle, for battle offers the greatest danger, thus requiring the greatest courage.

Today's readers tend to have difficulty reading Aristotle. But they find him difficult not because he places the hero at the center of the story: they take for granted that the story is about them. Neither do they particularly balk at the underlying assumption of violence—the emblematic role of the soldier: for they assume that in a world of limited goods, there is bound to be conflict at some stage so that good may prevail. No, what today's readers find most difficult about Aristotle is his assumption that, though everyone would want to be a hero, very few people will be, and that so being requires a Herculean effort of discipline and will. Today's readers object to such elitism. Democracy flattens out such distinctions. It dictates that everyone has the 'right' to be a hero, and it shouldn't be restricted to those with aptitude, effort, and skill. Because everyone can be a hero, the most mundane of activities and commitments and achievements may be regarded as heroic. The exception is the hero that makes a beautiful gesture abstracted from story—who forms a human bridge to help passengers escape a sinking ship, or rescues a child from the flames. Anyone can be a hero by making a spontaneous gesture. The point is not that these activities are highly regarded, but that everyone must have the right to be regarded as the center of his or her own story.

Aquinas did not seek to inspire his readers to be heroes. The virtues he commends are not those that enable his readers to make decisive interventions in the heart of battle or the height of controversy. The virtues he proposes are those that enable Christians to follow Christ. They are not called to be heroes. They are called to be saints. The word 'hero' does not appear in the New Testament. The word 'saint' occurs sixty-four times. What is the difference between a hero and a saint? Five differences present themselves.

To start with, there is a significant difference between the kind of story that is told about heroes and the kind of story that is told about saints. The hero always makes a decisive intervention at a moment when things are looking like they could all go badly wrong. The hero steps up and makes everything turn out right. In other words, the hero is always at the center of the story. By contrast, the saint is not necessarily a crucial character. The saint may be almost invisible, easily missed, quickly forgotten. The hero's story is always about the hero. The saint is always at the periphery of a story that is really about God.

Next comes the question of why the story is told. The hero's story is always told to celebrate the virtues of the hero. The hero's strength, courage, wisdom, or great timing: such are the qualities on which the hero's decisive intervention rests. By

contrast the saint may well not have any great qualities. The
saint may not be strong, brave, clever, or opportunistic. But the
saint is faithful. The story of the hero is told to rejoice in valor.
The story of the saint is told to celebrate faith.

Third, there is what the story takes for granted. The definitive heroic icon is the soldier, who is prepared to risk death for
the sake of a high good. The noblest death is death in battle, for
battle offers the greatest danger, thus requiring the greatest
courage. The story assumes that in a world of limited resources,
there is bound to be conflict at some stage so that good may
prevail. But saints assume a very different story. They do not
need to learn how to fight over competing goods, because
Christ has fought for and secured the true good, and the goods
that matter now are not limited or in short supply. Love, joy,
peace, faithfulness, gentleness—these do not rise or fall with
the stock market. The saint's story does not presuppose scarci-
ty; it does not require the perpetuation for violence. Whereas
the icon of heroism is the soldier, the icon of sanctity is the martyr. The soldier faces death in battle; the martyr faces death by
not going to battle. The soldier's heroism is its own reward: it
makes sense in any language that respects nobility and aspires
to greatness. The martyr's sanctity makes no sense unless
rewarded by God: it has no place in any story except that of
Christ's redeeming sacrifice and the martyr's heavenly crown.

Fourth, there is what happens when the story goes wrong.
The hero is at the center of the story. It is the hero's decisive
intervention that makes the story come out right. Without the
hero all would be lost. So if the hero makes a mistake, if the
hero bungles or exposes a serious flaw—it is a disaster, a catas-
trophe, probably fatal for the story and, if it is a big story,
possibly pretty serious for life as we know it. By contrast, the
saint expects to fail. If the saint's failures are honest ones, they
merely highlight the wonder of God's greater victory. If the
saint's failures are less admirable ones, they open out the cycle
of repentance, forgiveness, reconciliation, and restoration that
is what Christians call a new creation. A hero fears failure, flees
mistakes, and knows no repentance: the saint knows that light
only comes through cracks, that beauty is as much (if not
more) about restoration as about creation.

Finally, the hero stands alone against the world. The story of
the hero shows how he or she stands out from the community
by the excellence of his or her virtue, the decisiveness of his or
her intervention, or their simple right to have his or her story
told. The story of God tells how he expects a response from his
disciples that they cannot give on their own: they depend not
only on him but on one another for resources that can sustain
faithful lives, and they discover that their dependence on one
another is not a handicap but is central to their witness. Of
those sixty-four references to saints in the New Testament,
every one is in the plural. Saints are never alone. They assume,
demand, require community—a special kind of community,
the communion of saints. Heroes have learned to depend on
themselves; saints learn to depend on God and on the community of faith. The church is God's new language, and it
speaks not of a country fit for heroes to live in but of a com-
monwealth of saints.

That is why, if theological ethics is to tell a story that continues to be about God, it must concentrate on the narrative and
practice of the church and the witness of the saints.

Endnotes

1   An author who might be taken to epitomize the universal strand in
    contemporary Christian ethics would be Hans Küng. See, for exam-
    ple, his *A Global Ethic*, trans. John Bowden (London: SCM, 1997).
2   Among a wide range of titles, see for example Susan Frank
    Parsons, ed., *The Cambridge Companion to Feminist Theology*
    (Cambridge: Cambridge University Press, 2002); Gustavo
    Gutierrez, *A Theology of Liberation: History, Politics, Salvation*, rev. ed.
    (London: SCM, 1988); and Michael Northcott, *The Environment and
    Christian Ethics* (Cambridge: Cambridge University Press, 1996).
3   See for example Rosemary Radford Ruether, *Sexism and God-Talk:
    Towards a Feminist Theology* (London: SCM, 1983).
4   Adrian Hastings, *The Church in Africa, 1450–1950* (Oxford, UK:
    Oxford University Press, 1996).
5   Gustavo Gutierrez, *We Drink from Our Own Wells: The Spiritual
    Journey of a People*, trans. Matthew J. O'Connell (Maryknoll, NY:
    Orbis, 1990).

⁶ Richard L. Fern, *Nature, God and Humanity: Envisioning an Ethics of Nature* (Cambridge: Cambridge University Press, 2002).

⁷ I owe this understanding of Saint Antony to Brian S. Hook and R.R. Reno, *Heroism and the Christian Life: Reclaiming Excellence* (Louisville, KY: Westminster John Knox, 2000).

⁸ See John Howard Yoder, *The Christian Witness to the State* (Newton, KS: Faith & Life, 1964).

⁹ I discuss sectarianism at greater length in my *Transforming Fate into Destiny: The Theological Ethics of Stanley Hauerwas* (Carlisle, UK: Paternoster, 1998 now reprinted by Wipf & Stock), 90–125, and 141–50, where I see the issue as one of the triumphs of time over space. See also chap. 6 below.

¹⁰ A painful example of this is described vividly by Duncan Forrester in his treatment of the church at Dachau. See his 'The Church and the Concentration Camp: Some Reflections on Moral Community,' in Mark Thiessen Nation and Samuel Wells, eds., *Faithfulness and Fortitude: In Conversation with Stanley Hauerwas* (Edinburgh: T & T Clark, 2000), 189–207.

¹¹ It is significant that James Wm. McClendon begins his three-volume systematic theology with *Ethics*, in the place where philosophical theology might conventionally go, and ends with a volume on *Witness*, in place of a volume on philosophical theology and in the location in the series usually reserved for ethics. See his *Systematic Theology*, vol. 1, *Ethics*, 2ⁿᵈ ed. (Nashville: Abingdon, 2002) and James Wm. McClendon with Nancey Murphy, *Systematic Theology*, vol. 3, *Witness* (Nashville: Abingdon, 2000).

¹² For further exploration of heroes and saints, the violence of the nation-state, and the contrast between Aristotle's city-state and Augustine's church, see Samuel Wells, 'The Disarming Virtue of Stanley Hauerwas,' *Scottish Journal of Theology* 52/1 (1999): 82–88; Jean Bethke Elshtain, 'Citizenship and Armed Civic Virtue: Some Questions on the Commitment to Public Life,' in Charles H. Reynolds and Ralph Norman eds., *Community in America: The Challenge of Habits of the Heart* (Berkeley: University of California Press, 1988); and John Milbank, *Theology and Social Theory: Beyond Secular Reason* (Oxford, UK: Blackwell, 1990). There are also significant issues raised by Stanley Hauerwas and Charles Pinches in *Christians Among the Virtues: Theological Conversations with Ancient and Modern Ethics* (London: University of Notre Dame Press, 1997) and by Brian S. Hook and R.R. Reno in *Heroism and the Christian Life*.

Chapter 3

How We Lay Bricks and Make Disciples

Stanley Hauerwas

The statement of the problem is the problem

The church seems caught in an irresolvable tension today. Insofar as we are able to maintain any presence in modern society we do so by being communities of care. Pastors become primarily people who care. Any attempt in such a context for the church to be a disciplined and disciplining community seems antithetical to being a community of care. As a result the care the church gives, while often quite impressive and compassionate, lacks the rationale to build the church as a community capable of standing against the powers we confront.

That the church has difficulty being a disciplined community, or even cannot conceive what it would mean to be disciplined community, is not surprising given the church's social position in developed economies. The church exists in a buyer's or consumer's market, so any suggestion that in order to be a member of a church you must be transformed by opening your life to certain kinds of discipline is almost impossible to maintain. The called church has become the voluntary church, whose primary characteristic is that the congregation is friendly. Of course, that is a kind of discipline, because you cannot belong to the church unless you are friendly, but it's very unclear how such friendliness contributes to the growth of God's church meant to witness to the kingdom of God.

This attitude about the church was nicely illustrated by a letter in *The Circuit Rider* about The United Methodist Church. It read:

> United Methodism has been criticized roundly and at length for what it is not—not liturgical enough, not theological enough, not scriptural enough, not congregational enough, etc. I want to celebrate one ignored item not of United Methodism—namely, it is not harmful to religious people.
>
> In my work as a professor and parish minister, I have met all manner of people from other denominations whose minds and souls have been bent all out of shape by larger doses of rigor than many people can bear. Some folks have been given such high injections of some entities that their systems have developed a total immunity to the Christian religion.
>
> By contrast, even many of the people who leave United Methodism because of what it is not go on to lead happy and productive Christian lives as clergy and members of other denominations. Whatever they did not get in United Methodism, they did not get a permanent hatred of the Christian church or of its God.
>
> Wesley said it best. When asked what he intended to do with all those souls he was saving, he replied: 'I would make them virtuous and happy, easy in themselves, and useful to others.' Not a bad goal, Mr. Wesley! Not a bad record, United Methodism![1]

Such a letter no doubt describes not only United Methodism but the situation of many churches. As a result the church has increasingly found it difficult to maintain any kind of discipline that might make it identifiable as a distinct body of people with a mission to perform in the world. The church is very good at providing the kinds of services necessary to sustain people through the crises in their personal lives, but this simply reflects that fact that the church has become the privatized area of our culture. Of course, this has had an effect on the very notion of the pastoral office because the minister's authority is now primarily constituted by their ability to deliver pastoral services, rather than in liturgical leadership and the moral formation of the community.

The situation in which the church finds itself seems to make the activities of care and discipline incompatible. Care is identified with compassionate care of the individual and is now thought to be the first business of the church. Care requires understanding the particularities of the individual's situation so that the very idea of disciplining someone in a personal crisis is simply unthinkable. We seek to be understood and to understand—not to be judged.

In an attempt to respond to this set of circumstances, the primary strategy, at least for churches in the mainstream, has been to try to help people come to a better understanding of what it means to be Christian. Such a strategy assumes that what makes a Christian a Christian is holding certain beliefs that help us better understand the human condition, to make sense of our experience.[2] Of course no one denies that those beliefs may have behavioural implications, but the assumption is that the beliefs must be in place in order for the behaviour to be authentic. In this respect the individualism of modernity can be seen in quite a positive light. For the very fact that people are now free from the necessity of believing as Christian means that if they so decide to identify with Christianity, they can do so voluntarily.

When being Christian is construed in categories of self-understanding, with correlative senses of care, I fear that there is no way to recover a sense of the church as a community of discipline. Such an understanding of being Christian cannot help trying to cure our disease with more of the disease. The church cannot help become a life-style enclave and/or an umbrella institution where people are giving us the opportunity to associate with other people with their similar interests.[3] If we continue to follow the strategy that associates Christianity with certain beliefs or faith patterns I cannot see how we will, in any fashion, avoid the trend so acutely described by Wuthnow in *The Restructuring of American Religion* of people being members of churches in order to be associated with people with similar interests that are not in any way shaped by Christian convictions.[4]

When Christianity is understood fundamentally as a belief system necessary for people to give meaning to their lives, we cannot but continue to reinforce the assumption that salvation is for the individual. It is one of the ironies of our time that many of those who are identified with urging Christians to engage in politics in the name of their Christian beliefs hold what are fundamentally individualistic accounts of Christian salvation. They assume that Christianity entails social engagement, but salvation was still identified with the individual coming to a better self-understanding through the worldview offered by Christianity. The even greater irony is that the very form of society that was assumed to be the ideal for which Christians ought to work, namely a liberal democratic society, entailed the very presupposition that could only undercut any genuine conception of the social character of Christian salvation.[5]

In short, the great problem of modernity for the church is how we are to survive as disciplined communities in democratic societies. For the fundamental presumption behind democratic societies is that the consciousness of something called the *common citizen* is privileged no matter what kind of formation it may or may not have had.[6] It is that presumption that gives rise to the very idea of ethics as an identifiable discipline within the modern university curriculum. Both Kant and utilitarians assumed that the task of the ethicist was to explicate the presuppositions shared by anyone. Ethics is the attempt at the systemization of what we all, perhaps only inchoately, know or which we have perhaps failed to make sufficiently explicit.

Such a view of ethics can appear quite anticonventional, but even the anticonventional stance gains its power by appeal to what anyone would think upon reflection. This can be suitably illustrated in terms of the movie, *The Dead Poet's Society*. It is an entertaining, popular movie that appealed to our moral sensibilities. The movie depicts a young and creative teacher battling what appears to be the unthinking authoritarianism of the school in which he is teaching as well as his students', at first, uncomprehending resistance to his teaching method. The young teacher, whose subject is romantic poetry, which may or may not be all that important, takes as his primary pedagogical task to help his students think for themselves. Through great pedagogical sensitivity we watch him slowly awaken one student after another to the possibility of their own talents and potential. At the end, even thought he has been fired by the school, we are thrilled as his students found ability to stand against authority, to think for themselves.

This movie seems to be a wonderful testimony to the independence of spirit that democracies putatively want to encourage. Yet I can think of no more conformist message in liberal societies than the idea that students should learn to think for themselves. What must be said is that most students in our society do not have minds well enough trained to be able to think—period. A central pedagogical task is to tell students that they do not yet have minds worth making up.[7] Thus training is so important, because training involves the formation of the self through submission to authority that will, if done well, provide people with the virtues necessary to be able to make reasoned judgment.

I cannot think of a more conformist and suicidal message in modernity than that we should encourage students to make up their own minds. That is simply to ensure that they will be good conformist consumers in a capitalist economy by assuming now that ideas are but another product that you get to choose on the basis of your arbitrary likes and dislikes. To encourage students to think for themselves is therefore a sure way to avoid any meaningful disagreement. That is the reason that I tell my students that my first object is to help them think just like me.[8]

The church's situation I think is not unlike the problems of what it means to be a teacher in a society shaped by an ethos that produces movies like *The Dead Poet's Society*. Determined by past presuppositions about the importance of commitment for the living of the Christian life, we have underwritten a voluntaristic conception of the Christian faith, which presupposes that one can become a Christian without training. The difficulty is that once such a position has been established, any alternative cannot help appearing as an authoritarian imposition.

In this respect it is interesting to note how we, that is those of us in mainstream traditions, tend to think about the loss of membership by mainstream churches and the growth of so-called conservative churches. Churches characterized by compassion and care no longer are able to sustain membership, particularly of our own children. Whereas conservative churches that make moral conformity and/or discipline their primary focus continue to grow. Those of us in liberal churches tend to explain this development by noting that people cannot stand freedom, and therefore, in a confusing world devoid of community, seek authority. Conservative churches are growing, but their growth is only a sign of pathology.

Yet this very analysis of 'why conservative churches are growing' assumes the presumptions of liberal social theory and practice that I am suggesting is the source of our difficulty. The very way we have learned to state the problem is the problem. The very fact that we let the issue be framed by terms such as *individual* and *community*, *freedom* and *authority*, care versus *discipline*, is an indication of our loss of coherence and the survival of fragments necessary for Christians to make our disciplines the way we care.

For example, one of the great problems facing liberal and conservative churches alike is that their membership has been schooled on the distinction between public and private morality. Thus liberal and conservative alike assume that they have a right generally to do pretty much what they want, as long as what they do does not entail undue harm to others. The fact that such a distinction is incoherent even in the wider political society does little to help us challenge an even more problematic character in relationship to the church. Yet if salvation is genuinely social, then there can be no place for a distinction that invites us to assume, for example, that we have ownership over our bodies and possessions in a way that is not under the discipline of the whole church. For example, I was recently giving a lecture at a university that is identified with a very conservative Christian church. They were deeply concerned with the teaching of business ethics in their business school and had begun a lectureship to explore those issues. I was there giving a lecture called 'Why Business Ethics is a Bad

Idea.' I argued that business ethics was but a form of quandary ethics so characteristic of most so-called applied ethics. As a result, I suggested that business ethics could not help failing to raise the fundamental issues concerning why business was assumed to be a special area of moral analysis.

After I had finished a person who taught in their business school asked, 'But what can the church do given this situation?' I suggested to her that if the church was going to begin seriously to reflect on these matters, it should start by requiring all those currently in the church, as well as anyone who wished to join the church, to declare what they earn in public. This suggestion was greeted with disbelief, for it was simply assumed that no one should be required to expose their income in public. After all, nothing is more private to us in our lives than what amount we earn. Insofar as that is the case, we see how far the church is incapable of being a disciplined community.

However, one cannot help feeling the agony behind the questioner's concern. For if the analysis I provide to this point is close to being right, then it seems we lack the conceptual resources to help us understand how the church can reclaim for itself what it means to be a community of care and discipline. Of course, *conceptual resources* is far too weak a phrase, for if actual practices of care and discipline are absent, then our imaginations will be equally impoverished. What I propose, therefore, is to provide an account of what it means to learn a craft, to learn—for example—how to lay bricks, in the hope that we may be able to claim forms of care and discipline unnoticed but nonetheless present in the church.

Teach people how to lay bricks

To help us get a better picture of what it means for the church to be a disciplined community, we ought to learn how to lay bricks. This discipline will help us think about what it means to be saved, what it means to be a Christian. To learn to lay bricks, it is not sufficient for you to be told how to do it, but you must learn a multitude of skills that are coordinated into the activity of laying brick—that is why before you lay bricks you must learn to mix the mortar, build scaffolds, joints, and so on. Moreover, it is not enough to be told how to hold a trowel, how to spread mortar, or how to frog the mortar, but in order to lay bricks you must hour after hour, day after day, lay bricks.

Of course, learning to lay bricks involves not only learning myriad skills, but also a language that forms and is formed by those skills. Thus, for example, you have to become familiar with what a trowel is and how it is to be used. As well as mortar, which [American] bricklayers usually call 'mud'. Thus 'frogging mud' means creating a trench in the mortar so that when the brick is placed in the mortar, a vacuum is created that almost makes the brick lay itself. Such language is not just incidental to becoming a bricklayer but intrinsic to the practice. You cannot learn to lay bricks without learning to talk 'right.'

The language embodies the history of the craft of bricklaying. So when you learn to be a bricklayer you are not learning a craft *de novo* but rather being initiated into a history. For example, bricks have different names—for example, klinkers—to denote different qualities that make a difference about how one lays them.[9] These differences are discovered often by apprentices being confronted with new challenges, making mistakes, and then being taught how to do it by the more experienced.

All of this indicates that to lay bricks you must be initiated into the craft of bricklaying by a master craftsman. It is interesting in this respect to contrast this notion with modern democratic presuppositions. For, as I noted above, the accounts of morality sponsored by democracy want to deny the necessity of a master. It is assumed we each in and of ourselves have all we need to be moral. No master is necessary for us to become moral, for being moral is a condition that does not require initiation or training. That is why I often suggest that the most determinative moral formation most people have in our society is when they learn to play baseball, basketball, to quilt, cook, or learn to lay bricks. For such sports and crafts remain morally antidemocratic insofar as they require acknowledgment of authority based on a history of accomplishment.[10]

Of course, it is by no means clear how long we can rely on the existence of crafts for such moral formation. For example, bricklayers who are genuinely masters of their craft have become quite scarce. Those who remain command good money for their services. Moreover, the material necessary for laying bricks has become increasingly expensive. It has therefore become the tendency of builders to try as much as possible to design around the necessity of using bricks in building. As a result, we get ugly glass buildings.

The highly functional glass building that has become so prevalent is the architectural equivalent of our understanding of morality. Such buildings should be cheap, easily built, and efficient. They should be functional which means they can have no purpose that might limit their multiple use. The more glass buildings we build, the fewer practitioners of crafts we have. The result is a self-fulfilling prophecy: the more buildings and/or morality we produce that eliminate the need for masters of crafts and/or morality, the less we are able to know that there is an alternative.

In his Gifford Lectures, *Three Rival Versions of Moral Inquiry: Encyclopedia, Genealogist, and Traditions*, Alasdair MacIntyre develops an extensive account of the craft-like nature of morality. In contrast to modernity, MacIntyre argues that the moral good in not available to any intelligent person no matter what their point of view. Rather, in order to be moral, a person has to be made into a particular kind of person if he or she is to acquire knowledge about what is true and good. Therefore transformation is required if one is to be moral at all. In short, no account of the moral life is intelligible that does not involve some account of conversion. This is particularly true in our context, because to appreciate this point requires a conversion from our liberal convictions.

This transformation is like that of making oneself an apprentice to a master of a craft.[11] Through such an apprenticeship we seek to acquire the intelligence and virtues necessary to become skilled practitioners. Indeed it is crucial to understand that intelligence and virtues cannot be separated as they require one another. Classically this was embodied in the emphasis that the virtue of prudence cannot be acquired without the virtues of courage and temperance and courage and temperance requires prudence. The Circular or interdependent character of the relationship between prudence and courage suggests why it is impossible to become good without a master. We only learn how to be courageous, and thus how to judge what we must do, through imitation.[12]

Apprentices have to learn two distinctions before they can learn anything else.

> The first is the distinction between what in particular situations it really is good to do and what only seems good to do to this particular apprentice, but is not in fact so. That is, the apprentice has to learn at first from his or her teachers and then his or her continuing self-education, how to identify mistakes made by him or herself in applying the acknowledged standard, the standard recognized to be the best available so far in the history of that particular craft. Secondly, the apprentice must learn the difference between what is good and what is best for them with their particular level of training and learning in this or that set of particular circumstances and what is the good or best thing to do unqualifiably. That is, the apprentice has to learn to distinguish between the kind of excellence with which both others and he or she can expect of him or herself here and there, and the ultimate excellence which furnishes both the apprentice and the master craftsperson with their *telos* [goal, end, purpose].[13]

These distinctions are absolutely crucial if the teacher and apprentice are to be able to identify the defects and limitations of particular persons as they seek to achieve the *telos* of the craft. Habits of judgment and evaluation rooted in adequate and corrupt desires, taste, habits, and judgments must be transformed through being initiated into the craft. The apprentice must learn that there are some things that only the master can do, even though the apprentice might well accomplish what the master has done through luck. But luck or native talent is not sufficient to sustain the craft, so the apprentice must take the time to acquire the skills of judgment and accomplishment necessary for the achievement of the good.

So all crafts require that those who engage in the craft must come to terms with, and make themselves adequate to, the existence of some set of objects conceived to exist independent of their initial assumptions. Accordingly, there is a realist epistemological bias intrinsic to the crafts, but it is not the kind of correspondence theory that derives from the Enlightenment. The Enlightenment tried to show that the mind was immediately appropriate to a factual world without training. In contrast, our minds are adequate to that which we come to know only by being formed by the skills and practices of a tradition. Such training, of course, not only transforms us but transforms what it is that we think we need to know. That is why there can be no knowledge without appropriate authority.[14]

When the moral life is viewed through the analogy of the craft, we see why we need a teacher to actualize our potential. The teacher's authority must be accepted on the basis of a community of a craft which embodies the intellectual and moral habits we must acquire and cultivate if we are to become effective and creative participants in the craft. Such standards can only be justified historically as they emerge from criticisms of their predecessors. That we hold a trowel this way or spread mortar on tiles differently than on bricks is justified from attempts to transcend of improve upon limitations of our predecessors.

Of course, the teachers themselves derive their authority from a conception of perfected work that serves as the telos of that craft. Therefore, often the best teachers in a craft do not necessarily produce the best work, but they help us understand what kind of work is best. What is actually produced as best judgments or actions or objects within crafts are judged so because they stand in some determinative relation to what the craft is about. What the craft is about is determined historically within the context or particularistic communities.

MacIntyre points out that this temporal character of a craft stands in sharp tension with modernity's understandings of morality and truth. For it is modernity's presumption that any moral conviction or truth must be timeless. In contrast, the particular movement of rationality in a craft is justified by the history of the craft so far. 'To share in the rationality of a craft requires sharing in the contingencies of its history, under-standing its story as one's own, and finding a place for oneself as a character in the enacted dramatic narrative, which is that story so far.'[15]

A craft is never static. Thus masters are granted authority insofar as they exemplify in their work the best standards so far. What makes a master a master is that he or she knows how to go further, and especially how to direct others to go further, using what can be learned from tradition afforded by the past, so that he or she can move toward the *telos* of fully perfected works. The master knows how to link the past and the future, so that the *telos* of the craft becomes apparent in new and unex-pected ways. Therefore, it is the ability to teach others how to learn this type of knowing these skills through which the power of the master within the community of the craft is legit-imated as a rational authority.

For a craft to be in good condition, it has to be in a tradition in good order. To be initiated into craft is to be initiated into that tradition. But, as MacIntyre points out, such an initiation always involves at least two, if not more, histories. I come to the craft qua family member, qua community identity, qua training in other crafts. In order for my commitment to this craft to be intelligible, it must be understood in relationship to a hierarchy of crafts within a good community.[16]

I am not suggesting that we ought to think about becoming moral as an analogy to learning how to be a bricklayer, a pot-ter, or a teacher. Rather I am suggesting that learning to lay bricks or play basketball constitutes contexts in which we receive our most decisive moral training. As I argued in the second chapter, it is only the prejudice of modernity that would create a realm of morality abstracted from determina-tive practices like bricklaying, quilting, or gardening.

Moreover, it is just such an abstraction that makes it so hard for us to rightly conceive of disciplined care. To be initiated into a craft by a master certainly requires discipline, but it is the nature of such discipline that it is hardly noticed as such. That does not mean we may not be asked at times to learn to do things that seem to have no point, but in the doing of them we discover the point. When a craft and a community are in good working order, discipline is quite literally a joy, as it provides one with power—and in particular a power for service—that is otherwise missing.

On learning to be a disciple

But what does all this have to do with the church? First it reminds us that Christianity is not beliefs about God plus behaviour. We are not Christians because of what we believe, but because we have been called to be disciples of Jesus. To become a disciple is not a matter of a new or changed self-understanding, but rather to become part of a different community with a different set of practices.

For example, I am sometimes confronted by people who are not Christians but who say they want to know about Christianity. This is a particular occupational hazard for theologians around a university, because it is assumed that we are smart or at least have Ph.D., so we must really know something about Christianity. After many years of vain attempts to 'explain' God as Trinity, I now say, 'Well, to begin with we Christians have been taught to pray, "Our Father, who art in heaven . . .".' I then suggest that a good place to begin to understand what we Christians are about is to join me in that prayer.

For to learn to pray is no easy matter but requires much training, not unlike learning to lay bricks. It does no one any good to believe in God, at least the God we find in Jesus of Nazareth, if they have not learned to pray. To learn to pray means we must acquire humility not as something we try to do, but as commensurate with the practice of prayer. In short, we do not believe in God, become humble, and *then* learn to pray, but in learning to pray we humbly discover we cannot do other than believe in God.

But, of course, to learn to pray requires we learn to pray with other Christians. It means we must learn the disciplines necessary to worship God. Worship, at least for Christians, is the activity to which all our skills are ordered. That is why there can be no separation of Christian morality from Christian worship. As Christians, *our worship is our morality for it is in worship we find ourselves engrafted into the story of God.* It is in worship that we acquire the skills to acknowledge who we are—sinners.

This is but a reminder that we must be trained to be a sinner. To confess our sin, after all, is a theological and moral accomplishment. Perhaps nowhere is the contrast between the account of the Christian life I am trying to develop and most modern theology clearer than on this issue. In an odd manner Christian theologians in modernity, whether they are liberals or conservatives, have assumed that sin is a universal category available to anyone.[17] People might not believe in God, but they will confess their sin. As a result, sin becomes an unavoidable aspect of the human condition. This is odd for a people who have been taught that we must confess our sin by being trained by a community that has learned how to name those aspects of our lives that stand in the way of our being Jesus' disciples.

For example, as Christians we cannot learn to confess our sins unless we are forgiven. Indeed as has often been stressed, prior to forgiveness we cannot know we are sinners. For it is our tendency to want to be forgivers such that we remain basically in a power relation to those we have forgiven. But it is the great message of the gospel that we will only find our lives in that of Jesus to the extent that we are capable of accepting forgiveness. But accepting forgiveness does not come easily, because it put us literally out of control.

In like manner we must learn to be a creature. To confess that we are finite is not equivalent to the recognition that we are creatures. For creaturehood draws on a determinative narrative of God as creator that requires more significant knowledge of our humanity than simply that we are finite. For both the notions of creature and sinner require that we find ourselves constituted by narratives that we did not create.

As I indicated earlier, that is to put us at deep odds with modernity. For the very notion that our lives can be recognized as lives only as we find ourselves constituted by more determinative narrative that has been given to us rather than created by us, is antithetical to the very spirit of modernity. But that is but an indication of why it is necessary that this narrative be carried by a body of people who have the skills to give them critical distance to those of the world.

In some ways all of this remains quite abstract because the notions of 'sinner' and 'creature' still sound more like self-understanding rather than characteristics of a craft. That is why we cannot learn to be a sinner separate from concrete acts of confession. Thus in the letter of James we are told, 'Are any among you sick? They should call for the elders of the church and have them pray over them, anointing them with oil in the name of the Lord. The prayer of faith will save the sick, and the Lord will raise them up; and anyone who has committed sins will be forgiven. Therefore confess your sins to one another, and pray for one another, so that you may be healed. The prayer of the righteous is powerful and effective' (Jas 5:14–16). Such practice, I suspect, is no less important now as it was then. We cannot learn that we are sinners unless we are forced to confess our sins to other people in the church. Indeed it is not possible to learn to be a sinner without a confession and reconciliation. For it is one thing to confess our sin in general, but it is quite another to confess our sin to one in the church who we may well have wronged and to seek reconciliation. Without such confessions, however, I suspect we cannot be church at all.[18]

For example, when Bill Moyers did his public broadcast series on religion in America, the taping on fundamentalism was quite striking. He showed a fundamentalist pastor in Boston discussing a pastoral problem with one of his parishioners. The parishioner's wife had committed adultery and had confessed it to the church. After much searching and discussion, the church had received her back after appropriate penitential discipline. However, her husband was not ready to be so forgiving and did not wish to receive her back. The fundamentalist pastor said, 'You do not have the right to reject her, for as a member of our church you too must hold out the same forgiveness that we as a church hold out. Therefore I'm not asking you to take her back, I am telling you to take her back.'

I anticipate that such an example strikes fear in most of our liberal hearts, but it is also a paradigmatic form of what I take forgiveness to be about. In Boston one with authority spoke to another on behalf of the central skills of the church that draw their intelligibility from the gospel. There we have an example of congregational care and discipline that joins together for the upbuilding of the Christian community.

Of course, if the church lacks masters who have undergone the discipline of being forgiven, then indeed we cannot expect that such discipline will be intelligible. But I do not believe that we are so far gone to lack such masters. Indeed they are the ones who continue to carry the history to help us learn from our past so that our future will not be determined by the temptation to live unforgiven and thus unskillful lives.

Endnotes

[1] *The Circuit Rider* 24 (March, 1989), The letter was signed by Dennis Groh of Evanston, Illinois.

[2] I think Lindbeck's account of the experiential expressivist model in his *The Nature of Doctrine: Religion and Theology in a Post Liberal Age* (Philadelphia: Westminster Press, 1984) fails to give an adequate account of the material factors that make the experiential expressivist model so powerful. Experiential expressivism is almost required by the privatisation of people's lives that goes hand in hand with political liberalism and capitalist ecomony. Even more conservative denominations, therefore, in spite of what they may hold explicitly, end up in some form of experiential expressivism.

[3] The phrase *life-style enclave* I obviously have borrowed from Robert Bellah and his coauthors in their *Habits of the Heart: Individualism and Commitment in American Life* (Berkeley: University of California Press, 1985).

[4] Robert Wuthnow, *The Restructuring of American Religion: Society and Faith since World War II* (Princeton: Princeton University Press, 1988).

[5] The originator of this peculiar blend of Christian social action with individualistic accounts of Christian salvation was, of course, Reinhold Niebuhr. In an odd way Niebuhr moved away from the social gospel exactly at the wrong point, as he gave what was an essentially Lutheran understanding of salvation in opposition to the more Calvinistic strains of the social gospel. Niebuhr, in effect,

was the Lutheran law/gospel distinction in American pragmatic dress.

6   MacIntyre notes that the assumption of the eighteenth-century moralists was that there was a universality of moral agreement about fundamentals in ethics. They were not unaware, however, that often there were differences between cultures, but these differences were thought to derive from circumstances. This was combined with a belief in progress, so that some societies were obviously further along than others concerning more appropriate application of the basic rules which all shared. The purpose of moral theory in such a world is not just recording and protecting the judgments of the plain person, but the constructive text "of organizing and harmonizing the moral beliefs of plain persons in the manner best calculated to secure a rational sense from the largest possible number of such persons, independently of their conflicting views upon other matters. The moral philosopher's aim, then, is, or ought to be, that of articulating a rational consensus out of the pre-theoretical beliefs and judgments of plain persons." *Three Rival Versions of Moral Inquiry: Encyclopedia, Genealogy and Tradition* (Notre Dame: University of Notre Dame Press, 1990), pp. 176–77. Modern moral philosophy from this perspective is a necessary correlative to the attempt to develop democratic societies that organize people irrespective of their moral training. I suspect that is the reason why some are beginning to see more commonality between Aristotelianism and Christianity because in spite of their deep differences, they are both equally antidemocratic.

7   For a further development of this, see my "Honor in the University," *First Things* 10 (February, 1991), pp. 26–31.

8   I am aware that such a claim appears authoritarian, but ironically, I think it is just the opposite of authoritarianism. What does it mean to introduce students to think like me? It means I must introduce them to all the sources that think through me, but different from me as the different voices that think through me provide them with skills I have not appropriated sufficiently.

9   Klinkers were those bricks that were at the bottom of the kilns and they were therefore often overfired. They would sometimes have interesting projections that made quite beautiful walls. The difficulty with klinkers is they were extremely hard and therefore when you laid them, they could float on the mortar. Often bricklayers without much experience would find it very hard to lay klinkers because they were almost impossible to lay level over an

entire course. The relationship between the consistency of the brick and the consistency of the mortar is a matter to which brick-layers constantly have to adjust. For example, how you lay bricks at the midpoint of the day may be a bit different from how you lay bricks early in the morning, as the sun is not out in full force and the mortar does not dry out as quickly. So in the morning you might be able to spread your mud further along the course than you can at midday.

[10] George Will's *Men at Work: The Craft of Baseball* (New York: Macmillian Publishing Co., 1990) strikes me as a wonderful book in moral philosophy. The book really is about craft and how discipline is required to make the craft one's own. I must admit as I read through the book I thought I might catch Will distorting baseball by his own liberal presuppositions. The first chapters are primarily about individuals such as managers, pitchers, and hitters. However, Will clearly denotes the communitarian aspects of baseball in his chapter on the defense. It is a book well worth contemplating.

[11] MacIntyre suggests "Moral inquiry moves toward arriving at theoretical and practical conclusions about [particular] virtues. But one cannot learn how to move toward such a conclusion without first having acquired some at least of those same virtues about which one is inquiring and without therefore having first been able to identify which virtues they are and, to at least some minimal extent, what it is about them which makes these particular habits virtues. So we are threatened by an apparent paradox and an understanding of moral inquiry as a type of craft: only insofar as we have already arrived at certain conclusions are we able to become the sort of person able to engage in such inquiry so as to reach sound conclusions. How was this threat a paradox—recognizably a version of that posed at the outset by Plato and the *Meno* about learning in general—to be circumvented, dissolved, or otherwise met? The answer is in part that suggested by the *Meno*: unless we already have within ourselves potentiality for moving toward and achieving the relevant theoretical and practical conclusions, we shall be unable to learn. But we also need a teacher to enable us to actualize that potentiality, and we shall have to learn from that teacher and initially accept on the basis of his of her authority within the community of a craft precisely what intellectual and moral habits it is which we must cultivate and acquire if we are to become effective self-moved participants in such inquiries. Hence there emerges a conception of rational teaching

authority internal to the practice of the craft of moral inquiry, as indeed such a conception emerges in such other crafts as furniture making and fishing, where, just as in moral inquiry, they partially define relationships with master-craftsmen to apprentice." *Three Rival Versions of Moral Inquiry*, p. 63.

12 For my reflections on this circular account, see my "Happiness, the Life of Virtue, and Friendship: Theological Reflections on Aristotelian Themes," *Asbury Theological Journal* 45, no. 1 (Spring 1990), pp. 21–35.

13 MacIntyre, *Three Rival Versions of Moral Inquiry*, pp. 61–62.

14 MacIntyre's epistemological views are more determinatively developed in the latter chapters of *Whose Justice? Which Rationality?* (Notre Dame: University of Notre Dame Press, 1988). There MacIntyre says, "The original and most elementary version of the correspondence theory of truth is one in which it is applied retrospectively in the form of a correspondence theory of falsity. The first question to be raised about it is: what is it precisely that corresponds or fails to correspond to what? Assertations in speech are written, certainly, but there as secondary expressions of intelligent thought which is or is not adequate in its dealings with its objects, the realities of the social and rational world. This is a point at which it is important to remember that the presupposed conception of mind is not Cartesian. It is rather of mind as activity, of mind as engaging with the natural and social world in such activities as identification, reindentification, collecting, separating, classifying, and naming in all this by touching, grasping, pointing, breaking down, building up, calling to, answering to, and so on. The mind is adequate with objects insofar as the expectation which it frames on the basis of these activities are not liable to disappointment and remembering which it engages in enables it to return and recover what it had encountered preciously, whether the objects themselves are still present or not. The mind, being informed as a result of its engagements with the objects, is informed by both images which are or are not adequate—for the mind's purposes, re-presentation of particular objects or sorts of objects and by contrast which are or are not adequate re-presentations of the form in terms of which objects grasped and classified. Representation is not as such picturing, but re-presentation. Pictures are only one mode of re-presenting, and their adequacy or inadequacy in functioning as such is always relative to some specific purposes in mind. One of the great originating insights of tradition—constituted inquiries is that false beliefs and false

judgments represent the failure of mind, not of its objects. This falsity is recognized retrospectively as a past inadequacy when the
discrepancy between the beliefs of an earlier stage of tradition of
inquiry are contrasted with the world of things and persons as it
has come to be understood at some later stage. So correspondence
or lack of it becomes a feature of developing conceptions of truth.
The relationship of correspondence or lack of correspondence
which holds between the mind and objects is given expression in
judgments, but it is not judgments themselves which correspond
to the objects or indeed to anything else" (pp. 356–57). Of course,
the strength of MacIntyre's position is to deny the epistemological
starting point of the Enlightenment tradition. That is why he must
so starkly juxtapose traditions as the Augustinian-Thomistic tradition does not assume it must secure a starting point epistomo-
logically in order to begin reflection. Thus the very structure of the
Summa as a disputation rightly indicates there is no place to start.
This has deep implications for the style of philosophical and
theological work since it become crucial that we find a form that
unsettles the Enlightenment presumption that truth can be presented in a lecture and/or essay. Thus I just learn to write theology in a way that denies that theology can be systematic.

15 MacIntyre, *Three Rival Versions of Moral Inquiry*, pp. 64–65.
16 Ibid., p. 128. MacIntyre argues that philosophy necessarily must
    become the master craft if our hierarchies are to be rational. There
    I fear he and I may well be in disagreement, depending on what
    he means by philosophy since I necessarily must argue that theol-
    ogy, not philosophy, is in service to a community that ultimately
    must claim philosophy as a servant.
17 Again Reinhold Niebuhr is the great representative of this ten-
    dency in modern theology. There is no question, moreover, it was
    a powerful apologetic strategy as long as one could presume the
    lingering habits of a Christian civilization. However, those habits
    now seem to me to be gone for good and with good riddance. This
    issue again is nicely illustrated by Martha Nussbaum's review of
    MacIntyre's *Whose Justice? Which Rationality?* Titled "Recoiling
    from Reason," *New York Review of Books* 36, no. 19 (December 7,
    1989), pp. 36–41. In that review she accuses MacIntyre of intro-
    ducing the concept of sin to underwrite an authoritarian politics,
    and in this case a church, that cannot but offend any rational
    account of human existence. In contrast, Nussbaum argues that
    we must recover Aristotle without Christian eyes because only
    then are we capable of securing the kind of rational agreement

necessary to sustain modern liberal society. Thus she says, "This is not to minimize the difficulty of going beyond recognition of common experience in problems to construct common norms. With each step such an inquiry should balance the concrete experience of particular groups with an interest in what is common to all. How one might do this remains an immensely challenging question, but I see no reason to suppose that it cannot be done. If the doctrine of original sin, as MacIntrye interprets it, were true, the obstacles in the way of carrying out such would be formidable, since presumably original sin impedes the reasoning of each reasoned as well as making it difficult for a reasoned view to win acceptance. But MacIntyre has given us no good reason to believe that doctrine is true. And unless and until we accept some such idea we do not have reason to relax our demands for good reasons, deferring to authority" (p. 41). Though I think Nussbaum is wrong to assume that an account of sin is meant to underwrite an authoritarian politics, she is surely right to argue that those committed to the grand liberal project should reject any notion of sin. For a more extended discussion of Nussbaum see my "Can Aristotle Be a Liberal? Nussbaum on Luck," *Soundings* 72, no. 4 (Winter 1989), pp.675–92.

[18] One of the great problems after Protestantism lost the confessional was any ability to know how to name sins as sins. It is one of the great riches of the Catholic tradition that it is able to locate avarice, greed, lust, theft, adultery, and murder in a tradition that gives them a rational display as sin. As Protestants we have lost the ability to name our sins and thus lack the kind of discerning practices to have our lives located within the narrative of the church. For further reflections in this respect see my "Casuistry in Context," *Experience in Medicine*, ed. by Warren Reich (forthcoming).

Chapter 4

Carving Stone or Learning to Speak Christian

Stanley Hauerwas

Learning to be a stone carver

I was raised a bricklayer. Actually, that is not quite true. I was raised to labour for bricklayers. I eventually learned to lay bricks, but not with the skill of my father who was a master craftsman. In truth I was a better labourer than I was a brick-layer because to be a master craftsman requires years in the trade. It is important to remember, however, that while the labourer may not have the skill of the bricklayer no one can become a bricklayer, at least a bricklayer who is a craftsman, who has not learned to labour. For to lay bricks well requires that you have learned subsidiary skills such as how to mix mortar. Bricklaying, like all significant tasks, involves a hierar-chy of tasks requiring that those who would practice the craft learn those skills in an appropriate order.[1]

Attention to the training necessary for crafts such as laying bricks I believe is crucial if we are to understand the role the-ology might have in education, or, as I would prefer, moral for-mation. Too often I fear we associate education with teaching students how to think. We think, moreover, that thinking is a linguistic activity. Education certainly involves learning how to think and we do think linguistically, but it is important that we not think of thinking as something that goes on in our 'minds'. By observing the language two stone carvers use to reflect on their craft I hope to display why *learning to think*, as well as learning a language constitutive of thinking, *is rightly understood as work done with our hands.*

Such a view may seem quite odd in a conference designed to investigate what role theology, and in particular moral theology, may have in educating and forming lives.[2] Theologians are not usually associated with hard work or physical labour. I suspect theologians are more like labourers than bricklayers; that is, the theologian's task is to serve those who are masters of the craft of being Christian. Yet if that craft is constituted, as I think it is, by language, then it becomes all the more important that some are trained in the hard work of teaching the language of the craft. In particular it is crucial that those charged with the task of teaching not forget that teaching and learning a language, particularly the language of prayer, is as physical as learning to carve stone. A remark, however, I can only develop by saying more about learning a craft and, in particular, the craft of stone carving.

In *The Stone Carver: Master Craftsmen of Washington National Cathedral*, Marjorie Hunt tells the story of two Italian American master stone carvers—Roger Morigi and Vincent Palumbo.[3] These men were born and trained in Italy, but like other Italian carvers they came to America because they had skills necessary for the completion of buildings like the Cathedral Church of Saint Peter and Saint Paul in Washington, DC, which is more generally know as the National Cathedral of the American Episcopal Church.[4] Roger began work at the Cathedral in 1956 and was joined by Vincent in 1978.

Both Roger and Vincent were born into families of stone carvers. For them to be a stone carver was to be made part of a tradition whose habits of memory, the stories of carving stone, were inseparable from the stories of the family.[5] For example, as Vincent Palumbo carves he reports the memories of the years he spent being guided by his father noting:

> When I was working with my father on a job we don't feel we were father and son, but just partners. We talk a variation of things—how to do the best. He always teach me the secrets

how to give the master touch, how always he wants me—even if stone is dead material—still he was telling me how to make the stone look like life, almost talk, look realistic. Especially to give that small detail, so when we were carving flowers, the petals of the flowers look like moving. That was the best part. And I'm trying to do the best I can in his memory.[6]

Vincent and Roger take pride in their family tradition because they understand their families to represent the longer tradition of stone carving. To carve stone is to contribute to an ongoing tradition nestled within larger narratives that give purpose to the craft. That they are carving stone for a Cathedral means that they do not understand what they do to be just another job, but rather they participate in the story that constitutes their and our existence. Thus Vincent's claim that 'Even God gave Moses the ten laws on stone. He carved the Ten Commandments on stone. So this is the oldest trade in the world.'[7]

Roger was the master carver at the National Cathedral for twenty-three years. He reports it was a task he cherished about all others. 'To me,' he says, 'the Cathedral is like my home. Next to my home, it is home. When you say that, you say everything. You get attached to a place. This may be just stone to most people, but to me it's alive.'[8] Hunt reports that Roger's last carving for the Cathedral was a life-size statue of Adam. Roger's comment on his life work was, 'I finished where God began.'[9] That he would describe his work so wonderfully witnesses to his understanding of how his craft fits within a larger purpose.

Roger and Vincent were brought up in families of stone carvers, but they still had to be apprenticed to a master stone carver if they were to become masters of the craft. To be sure carving involves some formal instruction, but according to Roger you cannot teach anybody to carve. Rather

You give them the fundamentals of carving, like you take a hammer and a point and you hit, you take a chisel and cut. But the main thing in carving, you steal carving. When I say steal, you see, like you're in the shop and there are seven or eight apprentice boys. One would be a little better than the other, and you have two or three carvers working in the same place, so you watch one, you watch the other. Then you put it all together yourself. You develop your own technique.[10]

Roger and Vincent make clear, however, that within the community of stone carvers there is a clear and essential hierarchy determined on the basis of skill and seniority. They therefore describe their learning to be stone carvers as 'coming up' in the trade to indicate the long process required to work through the levels from apprentice and journeyman in order to finally become a master of the craft. Such a process is necessary because to be a good carver you need to be able to do everything associated with obtaining the stone from the quarry to putting the carved stone in place on the building. Thus a carver must be 'almost perfect as a stonecutter, which means you've got to be able to put a straight face on a slab of stone maybe two and a half meters long by a meter, meter and a half wide, with different kinds of tools—we call a six-teeth or an eight-teeth point.'[11]

For stone carvers apprenticeship is imperative, but the master, at least at the beginning, is not expected to pay his apprentice. As the apprentice improves the master may start to pay the apprentice, but again that is at the master's discretion. According to Roger and Vincent such an arrangement is more than fair: 'You have to consider this,' Roger says, 'the guy who taught you, what he gives you, he gives you a gift. And if you dedicate yourself enough to learn, to make something of it, he gives you a gift that nobody can steal from you. What he gives you money can't buy.'[12]

Though the apprentice learns by imitating the master, this imitation does not mean one slavishly copies the master's way of working. Rather one must develop, in Roger's words, 'something of your own'. Therefore the master 'should correct you if you make mistakes, but they should allow you to use your own techniques, what you think, what you feel about it.'[13] Those just beginning to learn, therefore, must travel to other shops of stone cutters in order to learn how to work with different materials and tools.

A good stone carver is, in a manner, forced to be innovative because they soon learn that every stone is different, requiring different tools.[14] So there is no one right way of carving in general, but rather the stone carver must be ready to do what works best for each particular stone. Roger reports his father used to tell him, 'If it works to wipe it with your ass, do that!'[15] Stone carvers must be ready to work with a wide range of material, but because it is their task to transform raw material into art, they hate nothing more than having to work on a poor grade of stone. If the stone is 'crumbly' in Vincent's words, 'it ruins your ambition because you work and work, and it don't come up too good.'[16]

The stone carver, therefore, must constantly adjust his tools to the stone. For example, Roger observes that pink Tennessee marble is 'sensitive' because 'it resents the tools' whereas Botticino stone is like 'working glass—it's sharp, it snaps like anything.' In contrast Carrara marble is the kind of material that every little hit with a chisel brings life.[17] This means that not only must the carver adjust to the stone, but he must know his tools well because if a tool is tempered too hard it will cut the stone, particularly limestone, too roughly.

And so the precarious nature of the craft, the constant need to rethink one's approach, means also that one learns to be a stone carver through talk. Vincent says he was nourished in the craft in his home and in the discourse of daily life. He describes it this way:

> When you come from a traditional family you learn from talking. What happened to me, we was in that trade. We was talking about work anytime; at breakfast, dinner, supper, most of the subject was work. Think about this stone, how we gonna do this, who was gonna do that, we gotta use this trick. So you're growing, and you listen, and your mind, it gets drunk with all those things, and then, when it comes time, you remember.[18]

Stories are, therefore, crucial for learning to carve stone. Through tales of personal experience and stories passed from one generation to another, stone carvers learn habits, attitudes, and standards 'that lie at the heart of who they are and what they do.'[19] The stories, moreover, name as well as constitute the virtues required to be a carver of stone. Vincent observes, to carve stone 'it requires 100 percent concentration' because, according to Roger, 'You've got to be patient and not overestimate the stone, because when you overestimate the stone, it comes back and bites you.'[20]

To learn to carve stone, therefore, is not like learning a language—to learn to carve stone is a language that is inseparable from the work itself. Hunt describes Vincent's formation as a child this way: 'like a child learning a language, Vincent began to acquire a grammar of stone carving; he began to piece together knowledge of the various elements of the craft and the underlying principles that governed them.'[21] In Vincent's words he learned the music of stone carving:

> I remember this clear, especially when I was young and I was there [in his grandfather's shop] trying to learn stonecutting. I remember we was about eight or nine stonecutters. We was three or four kids like me and then the old masters. As we say, all the work was done by hand. We gotta put a face on this big slab of stone with a brush hammer and things like that. And what happened while we were working one of the guys start to sing. While he's singing, all the rest they start singing too. And so what happened, we work by the tune of the music, of the singing. So we beat the bush hammer on the stone to make some kind of music; it was according to the singing. And we make more production because you can't stop, you can't split the singing. And it's many times like that.[22]

Vincent draws on the analogy of music to describe what he understands a stone carver to be, that is, a performer. Just as a composer can write a beautiful symphony it remains the case that the beauty of the symphony depends on it being played well by the musicians. So it is with carving. 'The sculptor makes a beautiful piece, but it's up to the carver to make the work on stone look really good or to ruin the thing because he does not know how to carve.'[23] According to Vincent stone carving is the art of reduction in which the carver brings into view what was hidden in the block of stone. But to reveal what was hidden, Vincent suggests, is miraculous. He puts it this way: 'The sculptor is the creator. He creates on clay. And then when they cast on plaster is the death. And the carving is the resurrection. That is the motto of our branch of the stone business.'[24]

What Vincent, Roger, and Alasdair MacIntyre have to teach us

If we are to recover a determinative understanding of the contribution theology might make for the formation of Christians I think we best think of education more like teaching people how to carve stone rather than what we usually associate with education provided by academic institutions.[25] This is particularly the case if education is about forming people in the habits of speech that make possible the virtues constitutive of the Christian tradition. The problem with the knowledge so often taught in our schools is that in such a setting Christian convictions cannot help but be presented as information. But information, by its very nature, is not meant to do any work and is thereby open to ideological distortions.[26]

That is why I think it important to make explicit what Vincent and Roger have to teach us—not only about how to carve stone but what is entailed in learning any significant way of life. They were fortunate, of course, to be born into families in which the tradition of stone cutting was, so to speak, in the air they breathed and in the food they ate. The habits of hard work were not foreign to them. Yet it was not sufficient for them to be born into families of stone carvers. In order to become master stone carvers it was necessary for them to become apprenticed to masters of the craft. Through their apprenticeships they acquired the more basic skills necessary to perform at the highest level of stone carving. In the process they learned to be patient because without patience they could not have learned how to carve the stone.

That apprentices acquire the virtues in the process of learning the basic skills of stone carving has important implications for how education should be understood. Not only should there be a clear hierarchy of skills into which the student is initiated, but those skills should habituate the student in a manner that they acquire power to do what otherwise they could not do. As a result students will be able to discover that knowledge, at least the knowledge associated with theology, requires that our lives be transformed. Such a transformation, however, is best understood retrospectively because the very virtues acquired in learning the story are necessary to understand what has happened to us. Thus the virtues require that we have become virtuous in order for us to recognize we have done so.

Education so understood happens through imitating a master. Yet the key to learning from a master is learning when it is appropriate to depart from what one has learned from the master. Innovation is necessary because no stone is the same nor is any significant story finished. In order to recognize the challenge, the difference this or that stone may present, the stone carver must learn the 'grammar of the stone'. Language is constitutive of not only the practice of stone carving, but any significant practice. Just as a master stone carver teaches his apprentice through the stories of the craft so any teacher must help the student learn how to say what they do. For the apprentice can only become a master by locating their lives in and through the narratives that have shaped their training.

To learn the language of stone carving is to learn to tell the stories constitutive of the trade. These stories make up the tradition of stone carving so that skills of stone carving can be passed on from one generation to the next. Still, the tradition of stone carving—like any significant tradition—changes, requiring that those in the tradition be articulate in order to insure the changes remain faithful to the work of stone carving.

Yet the tradition of stone carving gains its purpose and intelligibility from other stories and traditions. How the tradition of stone carving fits within these larger narratives will require ongoing discussion and argument. For it may turn out that some practices and stories may distort the very character of stone carving. It is, moreover, quite possible for stone carving to be put to the service of quite perverse purposes and traditions;

which is but an indication that stone carving is not self-validating.[27]

This brings me to what I think we must learn from Alasdair MacIntyre if we are to ascertain what Vincent and Roger have taught us. Of course, my account of what Roger and Vincent have to teach us has obviously been shaped by MacIntyre's Aristotelian understanding of the virtues. The virtues, according to MacIntyre, are dispositions to act in specific ways for definite reasons. The exercise of the virtues, however, is not only for the sake of the virtue, but also for enjoying the kind of life of which the virtues are constitutive. Therefore to understand how the life of virtue is also the best life means the virtues must be part of an ongoing tradition about the goods that constitute a life worth living.[28]

MacIntyre notes that there is an important analogy between the development of the capacity for right judgment about the good life and how capacities for right judgment are developed in more particular forms of activity with their specific standards of excellence. According to MacIntyre,

> Just as an apprenticeship in sculpture or architecture is required in order to recognize what excellent performance in these arts consists in, just as training in athletic skills in necessary to recognize adequately what excellence in athletic performance is, so a capacity for identifying and ordering the goods of the good life, the achievement of which involves the ordering of all these other sets of goods, requires a training of character in and into those excellences, a type of training whose point emerges only in the course of the training. Learning of this kind, as of other kinds, is what the uneducated, left to themselves, do not and cannot want: 'those engaged in learning are not at play; learning is accompanied by pain' (Aristotle, *Politics* VIII, 1230a29).[29]

According to MacIntyre, Plato and Aristotle thought a *polis*, a politics, was necessary to provide the context for the disciplines necessary for the acquisition as well as the ordering of the virtues. Yet it was also the case, according to MacIntyre, that Plato and Aristotle recognized that no such *polis* was available. The Academy and the Lyceum were their attempt to develop philosophical schools that might discharge the function of the *polis*. Yet no school can do the work of the *polis*. MacIntyre argues that the same situation that faced Plato and Aristotle also faces us. As a result we try to substitute something called 'education' for what only a tradition can do.[30] That is why stone carvers like Vincent and Roger are so important for MacIntyre. For as long as such people exist MacIntyre thinks we at leave have some examples left of what a virtuous tradition entails.[31]

Yet MacIntyre also argues that in the absence of a *polis* it is not possible to provide an account of the 'systematic forms of activity within which goods are unambiguously ordered and within which individuals occupy and move between well-defined roles that the standards of rational action directed toward the good and the best can be embodied.'[32] Which means no matter how much effort we may as Christians put into education, the education that results, if it is not shaped by the practices of the church, may reflect a quite different understanding of the world than that determined by the gospel. We may think as Christian educators, for example, we are teaching the language of the Trinity, but if that language is divorced from the habits and practices necessary for work to be done by the church the language will seem at best 'idealistic' and at worst useless to those whom we teach.

Learning the grammar of Christ

In his book, *The Nature of Doctrine: Religion and Theology in a Postliberal Age*, George Lindbeck helps us see the challenge before us by providing a typology of three theories of religion each of which entails an account of language. The cognitive-propositional type assumes that the language of doctrine corresponds in an unproblematic way with objective realities. The experimental-expressive type interprets religious speech as symbols correlative to and interpretations of feelings or attitudes characteristic of the human condition. A third approach, which has obviously informed the position I have taken in this chapter, Lindbeck calls the cultural-linguistic.

From a cultural-linguistic perspective religious faith is understood to resemble a language correlative to a way of life. To be a Christian from a cultural-linguistic point of view is not *like* learning another language, but rather *is* to learn another language.[33]

Lindbeck observes that the great strength of those who represent the experimental-expressive type, who are usually associated with theological liberalism, is that they attempt to make religion experientially intelligible to those who do not share the faith.[34] That project usually assumes some account of epistemological foundationalism in order to sustain an apologetic strategy aimed to show that religious language can be correlated with characteristics of the human condition that are allegedly universal. The task of the theologian, therefore, 'is to identify the modern questions that must be addressed, and then to translate the gospel answers into a currently understandable conceptuality.'[35] The difficulty, however, is that if such a translation project is successful it is not clear why you need the language of faith at all.[36]

As an alternative Lindbeck suggests that the very idea of 'translation' is a mistake. Rather what we need is a method that more closely resembles ancient catechetical practices. Instead of trying to describe the faith in new concepts, we should instead try to teach the language and practices of the faith. Lindbeck observes,

> This has been the primary way of transmitting the faith and winning converts for most religions down through the centuries. In the early days of the Christian church, for example, it was the Gnostics, not the Catholics, who were most inclined to redescribe the biblical materials in a new interpretive framework. Pagan converts to the catholic mainstream did not, for the most part, first understand the faith and then decide to become Christians; rather, the process was reversed: they first decided and then they understood. More precisely, they were first attracted by the Christian community and form of life. The reasons for attraction ranged from the noble to the ignoble and were as diverse as the individuals involved; but for whatever motives, they submitted themselves to prolonged catechetical

instruction in which they practiced new modes of behaviour and learned the stories of Israel and their fulfillment in Christ. Only after they had acquired proficiency in the alien Christian language and form of life were they deemed able intelligently and responsibly to profess the faith, to be baptized.[37]

Lindbeck notes that after Christianity became socially established this kind of catechetical process disappeared though similar results was obtained in diluted form through normal processes of maturation. This normalization is now part of the problem because people, at least people who inhabit the countries that once were in some general sense 'Christian', know just enough 'tag ends of religious language' to inoculate them from recognizing the transformation of life required to speak Christian. The grammar of people formed in this way is exemplified by statements, often heard in America, such as, 'I believe in Jesus is Lord, but that is just my personal opinion.'

The problem, therefore, becomes that the unchurched, as well as many who are churched, may think of themselves in this time 'after Christendom' as quite pious but *their piety does no work*. In Lindbeck's words, they are often 'interested in translations of the gospel into existential, depth-psychological, or liberationist language that articulates their latent Christianity,' but the language so translated does no work analogous to the language Vincent and Roger had to learn in order to become carvers of stone.[38]

Just as Vincent and Roger had to learn the language of stone carving to carve stone, Christians must learn the language of faith if we are to carve and thus to be carved to be Christ for one another and the world. Vocabulary is everything. Few tasks are more important in our day than teaching the language of the faith. But as we saw in the case of Roger and Vincent the language must be constitutive of the work to be done. It is not as if the language is a means to do the work, but the language is the work to be done. What we say as Christians cannot be separated from the practices of a people called 'church'.

One of the ways Christians have tried to articulate the relation between what we say and what we do is by drawing on the tradition of the virtues. That we have done so should not be surprising because speech itself is habit. To learn to speak Christian, to learn to speak well as a Christian, is to be habituated. Thus we are told we must speak the truth in love. The love that we believe necessary to make our words true is not a subjective attitude, but rather is to be formed by the habits of the community necessary for the church to be a true witness. That is the work our speech is to do. Part of the educational task of the church requires some to be set aside, you can call them theologians if you desire, in order to ensure the words we use do not go on a holiday.

For some time, many Christians and non-Christians alike, no longer believe that the words Christian use do any significant work. In such a situation some are tempted to think the task of the theologian is to develop theories of meaning to show that what Christians say makes some sense even though there is no work for the language to perform. In contrast I am suggesting the task of the theologian, who may or may not be a master carver but must at least know what it means to be a master carver, is to direct attention to those masters of the faith whose lives have been shaped by the grammar of Christ. Let us, for example, reflect on lives like Dorothy Day and Jean Vanier whose lives are unintelligible if Jesus is not the Lord.

I believe God, the master carver, is doing a new thing for his people in our time. The 'new thing' is not unprecedented if we remember that the story of Israel is also our story. For I believe, as Lindbeck suggests, that the social and political power of the church is being 'reduced', just as Israel was 'reduced,' so that what has been hidden might be revealed. For a church so 'reduced' education is not some further activity the church needs to do beyond being church. For to be Christians will mean that you cannot avoid discovering that, as we say in Texas, you 'talk different'. I am convinced, moreover, that those who discover the difference our speech makes will also find their lives have been made happy. For they have been given good work to do in a world increasingly determined by the belief that there is no good work to do.

Not least among the good work Christians have been given is prayer. All Christian speech is to be tested by the one work we have been given as God's creatures. We call that work 'liturgy.' which is the work of prayer. And when we, like Vincent and Roger, learn the joy of the work we have been given our work will be sung. Indeed the language of the Christian, the stories that makes us who we are, must be sung because the language of our faith is the very act of witnessing to the master who shared the gift: Father, Son, and Holy Spirit. Christian education begins and ends in the praise of God.[39]

Endnotes

[1]   I have more extensive account of laying brick as a model for learning to be a disciple in the previous chapter. My account of how learning to lay bricks might illumine moral formation drew on Alasdair MacIntyre's account of what it means to be trained in a craft to display the character of moral rationality in his *Three Rival Versions of Moral Enquiry: Encyclopedia, Genealogy, and Tradition* (Notre Dame: University of Notre Dame Press, 1990), pp. 63–68. My account of the stone carvers in this chapter continues to be informed by MacIntyre's account of the necessity of a master for an account of moral education as well as the innovative character of a tradition.

[2]   This chapter was written for a colloquium on the topic, 'The Way of Life: Education, a Challenge for Morality,' sponsored by the Pontifical John Paul II Institute in Rome, 2006.

[3]   Marjorie Hunt, *The Stone Carvers: Master Craftsmen of Washington National Cathedral* (Washington: Smithsonian Institute Press, 1999). All references to *The Stone Carvers* will appear in the text.

[4]   That the Cathedral is qualified by 'National' should be an embarrassment for any Anglican. Unfortunately that does not seem to be the case.

[5]   These are the kind of memories that W. James Booth calls 'thick memories,' that is, they are habits that are often non-explicit behaviours that constitute 'the geological deposit of enduring relationships. This habit-memory is itself a form of persistence of the past' (*Communities of Memory: On Witness, Identity, and Justice*. Ithaca: Cornell University Press, 2006, pp. xi–xii). Booth argues that, 'there is an intuition which belongs to the keeping of such forms of memory that they should be preserved and transmitted as a kind of bearing witness, as a debt owed to the community.

This obligation in certain respects is closely kindred to justice and might be described as a kind of indebtedness: what is owed within the context of an enduring community, an obligation incumbent on us as persons sharing a life in common' (p. xii). Witness is the word Booth uses to name this aspect of memory, that is, because we are members of persisting communities of accountability we must bear witness to both good and bad memories.

6   *The Stone Carvers*, p. 5.
7   *The Stone Carvers*, p. 3.
8   *The Stone Carvers*, p. 37.
9   *The Stone Carvers*, p. 37.
10 *The Stone Carvers*, p. 41.
11 *The Stone Carvers*, p. 68.
12 *The Stone Carvers*, p. 51.
13 *The Stone Carvers*, p. 72.
14 MacIntyre puts it this way: 'The authority of a master within a craft is both more and other than a matter of exemplifying the best standards so far. It is also and most importantly a matter of knowing how to go further and especially how to direct others toward going further, using what can be learned from the tradition afforded by the past to move toward the *telos* of fully perfected work. It is in thus knowing how to link past and future that those with authority are able to draw upon tradition, to interpret and reinterpret it, so that its directedness towards the *telos* of the particular craft becomes apparent in new and characteristically unexpected ways. And it is by the ability to reach others how to learn this type of knowing how that the power of the master within the community of a craft is legitimated as a rational activity' (*Three Rural Versions of Moral Enquiry*, pp. 65–66). Masters are often not the most talented in a craft. I suspect the reason many mediocre baseball players become managers is because they have had to study the game as well as learn the skills of the game more thoroughly than those who are naturally gifted.
15 *The Stone Carvers*, p. 71.
16 *The Stone Carvers*, p. 104.
17 *The Stone Carvers*, p. 105. Questions of 'idealism' and 'realism' would appear quite differently I believe if those concerned with such issues would attend to learning a craft. MacIntyre argues, for example, that 'it is from *within* the practice of painting in each case that shared standards are discovered, standards which enable transcultural judgments of sameness and difference to be made, both about works of art and about the standards governing

artistic practice and aesthetic evaluation' ('Colours, Cultures, and Practices,' in *The Tasks of Philosophy: Selected Essays*, Volume 1 (Cambridge: Cambridge University Press, 2006), pp. 47–48). MacIntyre argues, therefore, that colour names are not arbitrary, at least, they are not arbitrary if we are to account for a painter like Turner.

Andrew Moore puts it this way: 'Christians only ever have reality under a description. We know God as he gives himself to us in Jesus Christ and by his Holy Spirit grants us faith. So to say we have his reality under a description is emphatically not to imply that the description constructs a reality that would not be in existence without it. However it is to say that it is not possible for us to adopt a stance external to this (or any other) perspective so as to give a complete metaphysical description of the universe and its creator' (*Realism and the Christian Faith*. Cambridge: Cambridge University Press, 2003, p. 214).

18   *The Stone Carvers*, pp. 20–21.
19   *The Stone Carvers*, p. 56.
20   *The Stone Carvers*, p. 100.
21   *The Stone Carvers*, p. 21.
22   *The Stone Carvers*, p. 62.
23   *The Stone Carvers*, p. 97.
24   *The Stone Carvers*, p. 98.
25   Of course, it will be objected that universities are not in the business of teaching crafts. I am suggesting, however, that stone carving provides a fruitful analogy for helping us think through the pursuit of intellectual disciplines in the university. And yet by invoking analogy I by no means want to undermine the rigorous discipline and intellectual merit of learning a craft such as stone carving. Indeed I would argue that stone carving should be taught in universities where such a discipline would serve to teach and preserve a particular tradition.
26   By drawing our attention to stone carving, therefore, I am challenging the assumption that education is merely the transference of information from an 'expert' to a 'non-expert.' I am, thereby, calling into question the model of the university or school where the goods of 'knowledge' are obtained through students' acquisition of intellectual disciplines as though the mastering of a 'discipline' could be acquired through the pursuit of the isolated individual. This is not only a point about pedagogy, but rather speaks to the very character of knowledge that should be at the heart of any institution that claims to be Christian. No one has

made this case more forcefully than Peter Candler in his *Theology, Rhetoric, Manuduction, or Reading Scripture Together on the Path to God* (Grand Rapids: Eerdmans, 2006). By contrasting Aquinas's understanding of reading as participation in the life of God to modern modes of reading that isolate texts qua texts, Candler helps us see how current practices of reading distort the character of what is read. Candler argues, therefore, that the very form of the *Summa* makes clear that Aquinas understood theology not only as a craft but as a trade in which the student received from the hand of the master the bodily habits—none more important than speech—that would lead the student to God. Candler shows how crucial to Aquinas's understanding of the 'art of memory' was the role of memory shaped by the Eucharist in which time is quite literally a reenactment of the reality of the Passion (p. 151). Because theology as knowledge is rightly understood as 'the performance of the soul's return to God in the company of faith that it must refuse to be encyclopedic'—thus the open-ended character of the *Summa*. I am indebted to Carole Baker for this way of putting the matter.

27 Those familiar with Wittgenstein I suspect have realized that the account I am giving draws on his example of 'Slab' in *Philosophical Investigations*, translated by G.E.M. Anscombe (New York: Macmillan, 1953), pp. 19–21. This part of the *Investigations* has been commented on by Rush Rhees in his 'Wittgenstein's Builders—Recapitulation' in *Wittgenstein and the Possibility of Discourse*, edited by D.Z. Phillips (Cambridge: Cambridge University Press, 1998) pp. 178–97. Rhees argues that Wittgenstein used 'Slab' to show the connection between the use of language and what people are doing, but Wittgenstein was wrong if, as he seems to suggest, giving orders of one sort or another might be the entire language of a tribe. Rhees acknowledges it is possible to imagine a people with such a limited vocabulary yet 'the trouble is to imagine a people who had a language at all and yet never spoke apart from times when they happened to be on this kind of building job.' Rhees observes, 'I do not think it could be speaking a language' (p. 182). In his *Ethics as Grammar: Changing the Postmodern Subject* (Notre Dame: University of Notre Dame Press, 2001), Brad Kallenberg defends Wittgenstein against Rhees arguing that Wittgenstein's understanding of language achieves the nuance Rhees suggests is needed (p. 47).

28 Alasdair MacIntyre, *Whose Justice? Which Rationality?* (Notre Dame: University of Notre Dame Press, 1988), p. 109.

29 MacIntyre, *Whose Justice? Which Rationality?*, p. 110.

30 For MacIntyre's most developed understanding of the role of 'education' see his 'Aquinas's Critique of Education: Against His Own Age, Against Ours,' in *Philosophers on Education: Historical Perspectives*, edited by Amelie Rorty (London: Routledge, 1998), pp. 95–108. MacIntyre's remarks in this essay on the relation between philosophy and theology are particularly interesting given his insistence that philosophy must maintain an independence from theology. He does say, however, that philosophers do have to learn from theology the limitations of their mode of inquiry (p. 101), which has important implications for education given Aquinas's views. For according to MacIntyre given Aquinas's understanding of the aims of education to involve training in virtues to achieve the goods, a good education cannot be supplied only by schools and universities. Rather cooperation is required between family, households, schools, and local political communities. This does *not*, however, mean that there must be a theological agreement between home, school, and political community, but rather an agreement is required concerning the practice of the virtues, an agreement that is independent of religious belief (pp. 105–6). One may wonder if this last conclusion is consistent with MacIntyre's understanding of the unity of the virtues. What is clear is that MacIntyre thinks Aquinas's understanding of education as formation in the virtues to acknowledge a good that is not chosen is at odds with education in America that 'takes it for granted that there is no such thing as *the* human good, but that each individual must at some point choose for her or himself among a variety of different and rival conceptions of the good. A good education is then an education that prepares individuals for making such choices. And by that standard a Thomist education is a bad education' (p. 107).

31 MacIntyre, *Whose Justice? Which Rationality?*, p. 99. See for example MacIntyre's account of the 'plain person' in his 'Plain Persons and Moral Philosophy: Rules, Virtues, and Goods,' in *The MacIntyre Reader*, edited by Kelvin Knight (Notre Dame: University of Notre Dame Press, 1998), pp. 136–52. MacIntyre argues that the 'plain person' is a proto-Aristotelian because every human being lives out their life in a narrative form structured by a *telos*. He argues that even philosophical alternatives that reject such a view of the 'plain person' are still informed by it. Kwame Anthony Appiah has recently argued that MacIntyre's understanding of the importance of narrative is not foreign to the kind

of liberalism represented by John Stuart Mill, *The Ethics of Identity* (Princeton: Princeton University Press, 2005), pp. 22–23.

[32] MacIntyre, *Whose Justice? Which Rationality?*, p. 141. These issues involve the vexed question of the unity of the virtues. In *Whose Justice? Which Rationality?* MacIntyre acknowledged he was wrong to criticize Aquinas's understanding of the unity of the virtues in *After Virtue* (p. x). For a good discussion of the significance of this change in MacIntyre's position see Christopher Stephen Lutz, *Tradition in the Ethics of Alasdair MacIntyre: Relativism, Thomism, and Philosophy* (Lanham: Lexington Books, 2004), pp. 101–4.

[33] George Lindbeck, *The Nature of Doctrine: Religion and Theology in a Postliberal Age* (Philadelphia: The Westminster Press, 1984), pp. 16–18. Lindbeck's book appear four years before MacIntyre's, *Whose Justice? Which Rationality?*, so he could not have anticipated MacIntyre's extremely important account of translation. Lindbeck's case, I believe, can be strengthened by MacIntyre's argument that there is no such 'language as English-as-such or Hebrew-as-such or Latin-as-such' (p. 373). Rather there is only Latin as written or spoken in the Rome of Cicero. Therefore MacIntyre does not deny that translation is possible, but he does deny that it is possible to translate a language in use (p. 387). To learn a language in use requires we learn to be speakers of a second first language (p. 375). I take it that what it means to be a Christian is to be committed to becoming an adequate speaker of a second first language called Christian—a language that in the learning teaches me how much I have to learn.

[34] Lindbeck, *The Nature of Doctrine*, p. 129. Paul De Hart has recently challenged Lindbeck's (and Frei's) attempt to draw a strong contrast between liberalism and postliberalism. In the process he provides a very useful contrast of Lindbeck's and Frei's agenda. De Hart's argument I think very successfully exposes the limits of Lindbeck's and Frei's typologies, but I think both Lindbeck and Frei rightly understood their work to be in discontinuity with most of the presumptions of liberal Protestantism. See Hart, *The Trial of Witnesses: The Rise and Decline of Postliberal Theology* (Oxford: Oxford University Press, 2006). That said, I have never had a stake in being a postliberal.

[35] Lindbeck, *The Nature of Doctrine*, p. 132.

[36] I will not deal with the cognitive-propositional type because I do not think it necessary for the position I am trying to develop.

[37] Lindbeck, *The Nature of Doctrine*, p. 132.

[38] Lindbeck, *The Nature of Doctrine*, p. 133.
[39] No one has argued this as well as Julian Hartt in his book, *Theology and the Church in the University*, Foreword by Stanley Hauerwas (Eugene: Wipf and Stock, 2006). Hartt's book was first published in 1968.

Chapter 5

On Developing Hopeful Virtues

Stanley Hauerwas and Charles R. Pinches

Therefore, since we are justified by faith, we have peace with
God through our Lord Jesus Christ. Through him we have
obtained access to this grace in which we stand, and we rejoice
in our hope of sharing the glory of God. More than that, we
rejoice in our sufferings, knowing that suffering produces
endurance, and endurance produces character, and character
produces hope, and hope does not disappoint us, because
God's love has been poured into our hearts through the Holy
Spirit which has been given to us.

Romans 5:1–5. RSV

Virtue talk and the Bible

It is a fair question to ask whether virtue language fits with
what the New Testament tells us. As our colleague and teacher
John Yoder has often reminded us, the New Testament seems
to speak more about what we can and cannot do than it does
about the virtues we ought to have. Even in texts like Galatians
5 where Paul speaks of virtues such as love, joy, peace,
patience, kindness, goodness, faithfulness, gentleness, and
self-control, he does so only after forbidding the works of the
flesh, namely, immorality, impurity, licentiousness, idolatry,
sorcery, enmity, strife, jealousy, anger, selfishness, dissension,
party spirit, envy, drunkenness, carousing, and the like. The

force of this second list, its length, and its ordinal priority to the list of the virtues (not to mention what it implies about the human condition) may suggest that instead of dwelling on the more affirming—and less specific—virtues we ought to attend to rules and law. This point can be made more forcefully when one considers the fact that when Christians read and study the New Testament as a guide to their lives, they discover therein both the admonition and the stories to support loyalty to a concrete person rather than to a set of abstract dispositions, such as the virtues may appear to be.

It is in this light that we will consider at some length in this chapter the opening quotation from Romans 5. In its shadow we will argue that the virtues do in fact express central aspects of the Christian life. It also suggests to us possible answers to certain questions about the distinctiveness of the Christian virtues and how that distinctiveness might relate to the peculiarity of the Christian story. As we offer these suggestions, we intend as well to reflect on more general questions of 'human nature' and how an understanding of it might relate to the story Christians tell.[1]

On the first matter, that regarding the Bible and virtue, the text from Romans is intriguing, since virtue talk lies so close to its surface. Suffering is not a virtue in itself, but it is related to virtue, and endurance, character, and hope seem to name dispositions that most of us would think of as virtues. Taken by itself, then, the text seems to give virtue a boost. But, as Yoder might remind us, no biblical text stands by itself. Glancing around (the text's surroundings are in fact quite well known), we see that this little bit of virtue talk is settled comfortably in the middle of some of the most profound and forceful reflections ever written about justification by faith.

This proves very interesting. For fidelity to justification by faith has been one of the strongest reasons why many in the Christian tradition have objected to the primacy of virtue language for displaying the nature of the Christian life. The objection has been put in two related ways. First, justification implies that the new life of grace comes to us as a free gift of God. Talk of virtue, on the other hand, seems to assume that the moral life is a kind of human achievement. Indeed, the forgiveness that is so crucial to the Christian understanding of justification seems to strike at the very heart of an ethic of virtue. Consider, for example, Aristotle's man of virtue. As we have suggested, his whole purpose seems to be to live in such a way that he need not be forgiven of anything. By giving favours rather than receiving them he insures his invulnerability to a love that might render him dependent. In contrast, unearned justification of the sort Paul expounds cannot but make those who receive it dependent upon the one who offers it as a free gift.

Second, an emphasis on justification seems to make reference to growth and development in the moral life suspect; by contrast, any virtue account seems required to highlight it. To build on the previous point, emphasis upon growth appears to imply achievement, even *self*-justification. When we set about to acquire virtue and when we believe we can and do make progress, we are inevitably tempted to believe in our own power to know and do what is right. Yielded to, this temptation cannot but deafen us to the true command of God.

It is hardly surprising that Karl Barth has put the point at issue in its starkest form. As he says,

> the relation between God and man is not that of a parallelism and harmony of the divine and human wills, but of an explosive encounter, contradiction and reconciliation, and which it is the part of the divine will to precede and the human to follow, of the former to control and the latter to submit. Neither as a whole nor in detail can our action mean our justification before God . . . Our sanctification is God's work, not our own. It is very necessary, therefore, that there should be the encounter, the confrontation of our existence with the command of God.[2]

Barth is well known for his emphasis upon the command of God (. . . we suggest . . . commands are indeed crucial to the Christian life, although we receive them best when our obedience is constitutive of our virtues). Command language fits well with a certain understanding of justification. From such a perspective the Christian life appears as a series of responses to particular commands, without the response implying a lasting effect in those who are commanded. There is continuity in the commands, but it is provided by the character of the commander, not the commanded. For Barth, therefore, the fundamental image for the Christian life is not growth, but repetition. Only God's command is capable of such repetition, for the

> repetition and confirmation of all other commands is limited: partly because, so far as content is concerned, they aim only at individual temporally limited achievements; partly because they aim at attitudes and therefore at usages which once they are established need no new decision. But the necessity as well as the possibility of repetition and confirmation of the command of God is without limit. Even if it aims at definite achievements and attitudes and actions and usages it always aims beyond them at our decision for Jesus, and just in this substance the decision demanded by God's command is of such a kind that it can and must be repealed and confirmed.[3]

Gilbert Meilaender has characterized this construal of the Christian life as essentially dialogical. The Christian life has a distinctive nature but no clear progression. It is a 'going back and forth, back and forth. That is to say, the Christian is simply caught within the dialogue between the two voices with which God speaks: the accusing voice of the law and the accepting voice of gospel. Hearing the law, we flee to the gospel. Life is experienced as a dialogue between these two divine verdicts, and within human history one cannot escape that dialogue or progress beyond it.'[4]

'Going back and forth, back and forth' implies movement, but not necessarily growth, which is the point at stake. Movement in a journey, however, does imply growth—although what kind remains open for specification. (For example, as we discussed earlier, a journey's destination is not fixed so clearly as a trip's. On a trip, we know where we are headed, and so how far we are from reaching it, something the very character of a journey precludes.) Since we have emphasized the metaphor 'journey' for the moral life, we are committed to the genuine possibility of growth and development—as we suppose anyone who uses the metaphor must be.

Meilaender himself speaks of journey, although with quali-
fication. 'Righteousness . . . consists not in right relation with
God but in becoming (throughout the whole of one's character) the sort of person God wills us to be and commits himself
to making of us. Picturing the Christian life as such a journey,
we can confess our sin without thinking that the standard of
which we fell short, in its accusation of us, must lead us to
doubt the gracious acceptance by which God empowers us to
journey toward his goal for our lives.'[5] Meilaender proposes
journey only after proposing dialogue and then recommends
that we hold both together, despite their obvious differences,
purposely refusing to resolve them. 'The tension between
these two pictures of the Christian life cannot be overcome,
nor should we try to overcome it.'[6] This outcome fits well within Meilaender's faithful Lutheranism; less faithfully, we no
doubt appear to leave justification behind in emphasizing
sanctification and the virtues it makes available.

This is an appearance we hope to dispel. To begin, it is
important to distinguish genuinely Christian notions of growth
in the moral life from the view (to which Christians have often
been tempted) that our moral development 'unfolds' from
what is in us naturally as potential. Growth in Christian virtue
is hardly an inevitable movement to the higher and better, nor
are the virtues the result of the development of a teleology
intrinsic to human nature. This is not to say our growth has
nothing to do with our 'nature'; with Aquinas we hold that the
kind of individual nature each of us has must inform how our
virtues are determined. Rather, the view we wish most to reject
is that suggested by Edmund Pincoffs when he states what to
him seems obvious, that 'a just man is a just man. He needs no
imprimatur to show forth what he is. Courage is no more a
Catholic than it is a Buddhist virtue; honesty commends itself
to Presbyterian and Coptic Christian alike.'[7] To the contrary, we
hold that just as a Calvinist unbeliever is different from a
Catholic unbeliever, the courage of a Christian is different from
that of a Buddhist. No appeal to human nature is sufficient to
insure the commonality of all human virtue. Instead, as
Alasdair MacIntyre has emphasized, any account of the virtues
requires a teleological understanding of human existence

articulated through a community's narrative.[8] For our purposes, the significance of this point is that an account of growth in Christian virtue cannot be generic. If, contra Pincoffs, all virtues are not the same, that the 'just person' is *not* everywhere and always recognizable as the 'just person,' then the account of how someone came to be virtuous or just will need to be placed in relation to the particular sort of virtues she has come to have.

What has this to do with our text from Romans and Paul's long discussion of justification in which it is placed? Suppose we fix on what is perhaps the most rudimentary notion of justification imaginable: by justification we are made just before God. As Paul makes plain, something decisive has occurred in Jesus that has changed our status as God sees us. Put this way, we can see that 'justification' begs for narrative display: what were we before, what are we now, and where is this change taking us?

Reference to narrative gives us room to note briefly that recent scholarship has done much to recover the centrality of apocalyptic eschatology in Paul's theology, or, to put it contentiously, to rescue him from the Lutherans. As J. Christiaan Beker notes,

> Paul's proclamation of Jesus Christ (= the Messiah) is centered in Paul's specific view of God and in a salvation-historical scheme. What does this mean? It expresses the conviction that, in the death and resurrection of Jesus Christ, the Covenant-God of Israel has confirmed and renewed his promises of salvation to Israel and to the nations as first recorded in the Hebrew Bible. These promises pertain to the expectation of the public manifestation of the reign of God, the visible presence of God among his people, the defeat of all his enemies, and the vindication of Israel in the gospel. In other words, the death and resurrection of Jesus Christ manifests the inauguration of the righteousness of God.[9]

As we hold, Paul's emphasis upon justification, and virtually all else he says, is incomprehensible apart from his eschatology. Eschatology names the narrative of God's salvation appropriated by hope—the key term in Romans 5:1–5. It is true, crucially true, that justification is a gift, a point that reminds us that the hope by which we journey is not of our own making. Far from arising from our own worthiness, our hope comes as an open invitation to locate our lives in a new history that is made present in the life, death, and resurrection of Jesus Christ.

Hope, forgiveness, and suffering

It is an important and largely unexplored question as to what the relation may be between Paul's eschatology and the teleology insisted upon by MacIntyre. Put abstractly, the question concerns the relation of nature (teleology) to history (eschatology) and would require consideration of the relation of happiness to suffering. In lieu of a full inquiry we will say what we suspect: as formed in Aristotle, MacIntyre's teleology, while explored (of necessity) in a tradition and therefore in relation to a community, need not end in community. In contrast, this is a requirement of Christian eschatology, which looks toward the communion of all the saints. Only within this eschatological framework can the Christian virtues receive full display.

Aristotle's teleology is necessarily based in some form of naturalism. That is, it will suppose that there is some common human nature which can be fulfilled or frustrated. This provides an important benchmark for the virtues. Insofar as we share a nature we will share virtues, that is, if we live a fully human life. This need not be all the virtues, for flourishing occurs in a concrete life, and the circumstances and environments of our various lives will differ. But *qua* humans we cannot have completely different sets of virtues, as one might suppose there would be an entirely different set of virtues for some nonhuman species of being with different capacities and a different *telos*.

Christian eschatology is less clearly bound by this requirement of nature, not the least because Christianity imagines a new world in which we all will be changed. It remains an open question, then, whether and how Christian virtues compare to the virtues others will claim.

At the very least, the comparison is tricky, as Robert Roberts has helpfully noted. In an attempt to find some commonality between virtues irrespective of their communal and traditioned context, Roberts suggests that the virtues have a grammar, a set of rules embodying a system of relation. For example, the structure of gratitude requires the reception of a nonobligatory good from another person; this is true of gratitude wherever it is found.[10] If this is true, and it surely seems plausible, some formal parallel might reasonably be drawn between the various historic virtue traditions.

As to the material implications of this formal point, however, we remain somewhat agnostic. No doubt there are some things we all share as humans: we all are embodied beings and as such have certain common material needs, most if not all of us live with a knowledge of our death, and so on. From this it likely follows that there is something like eternal questions for humankind which arise out of a 'human condition' that is, at the very least, a condition of neediness. However, registering this point must not blind us to the crucial importance of the way in which these questions are put. For instance, while it is true that 'naturally' we share a weak, needy, or fallible nature, from the perspective of the Christian gospel this is not the deepest truth about our human nature. We are, rather, fundamentally sinners for whom Christ died. And, contrary to Reinhold Niebuhr, sin is by no means self-evident; Christians and Jews know of it only by the story given in their peculiar history.

We do not think it is accidental that the diagnosis of our sinful condition is the burden of much of what Paul writes in Romans prior to chapter 5. 'All have sinned and fall short of the glory of God' (Rom 3:23), he says, a point that melds in the next verse with the assertion that justification comes to all 'by God's grace as a free gift, through the redemption that is in Christ Jesus.'

If one should wish to say that Paul is implying that sinfulness is 'natural,' since it is universal, we have no reason to quarrel. Knowledge of sin, and of God's forgiveness of it is, however, another matter. Indeed, as Paul goes on to claim, Jews are advantaged over others precisely because their law, which arose as God came to share their history, allows them to tell their story, and the story of the world, as one of sinfulness. Sin and redemption, while universal, are imbedded in a particular history, one we must come to share if we are to know our true state.

Roberts perceives this point as he considers how a grammar might be discovered among the Christian virtues. As he says, it may seem improbable that a virtue's grammar, as a formal notion, could be built on a historical belief. Nevertheless,

> the doctrine of righteousness through Christ's atoning death for sinners is the hub of the Christian view of the world, the axis upon which everything else turns. And the virtue of forgiveness is especially close to the hub. So in this case, like it or not, a particular historical belief is essential to the grammar of a virtue, and every exposition of Christian forgiveness must give a central place to this belief, just as every instance of distinctively Christian forgiveness involves envisioning the offender in the light of the cross. To put this in the terms of the Christian virtues-system, the historical fact that Christ died for sinners became an essential feature of human nature.[11]

Roberts's comments help us make an important epistemological point about the nature of Christian claims about 'our natures.' As he notes, there is an essential feature about our nature—a natural fact—that Christians claim is disclosed in a particular history. (Whether it might also be disclosed in another particular history is something Christians need not initially address, although by no means must they, nor should they, eliminate the possibility.) This feature about us comes in the Christian story with our need for justification—we learn of both together. It follows, then, that our instruction in our sin and in our redemption of necessity brings us within the narrative that sustains the Christian virtues. For example, the closeness of forgiveness to the hub of the Christian virtues depends upon the importance of the part of the story that tells us of our sin, and of our justification through the gift of God's son. This story, as we allege, is upheld by a Christian eschatology which itself implies the centrality of hope.

With this in mind, we see no reason to hold that there is an unresolveable tension between justification and the virtues of hope. Indeed, Christian hope, like sin, is something we must learn of as we come to share in a story which teaches us both why hope is essential and why it can be had at all. Furthermore, that the answer to our sin is the free gift of redemption in Christ focuses our hope: its source is in the God who forgives us, and its object is this forgiveness, which responds to our deepest need, of which we have lately learned. All hope relates to a felt need; if we have attained all that we might, there is nothing to hope in. Therefore, our knowledge of what we lack cannot but affect that for which we hope. If we return again to the question about our 'nature,' the knowledge that we are weak, dependent, or fallible is easily attained—as easily as the knowledge that we suffer. A 'natural' or generic hope can arise in relation to this knowledge, namely that we will be cared for and loved. This hope may prove a seed of new life, not only because it is grounded in a truth about our need for love but because, rather than attempting to deny or transcend fragility by grasping at power, it looks beyond itself for help from another. Yet defined merely in this way, 'naturally' we hope more for acceptance than for forgiveness. No doubt we are accepted by God as he forgives us, but precisely because it is an acceptance of forgiveness it is truthful in a way that mere acceptance without forgiveness is not—and the reason for this is that we are, in fact, sinners. Concomitantly, as Roberts notes, the gratefulness that can be found in certain other grammars of virtue is subtly changed within the Christian grammar. Phenomenologically, gratefulness is appropriately offered to someone stronger on whom we depend, or to someone who loves us despite our weaknesses. Yet this gratefulness will not be the same as that offered by those who have been forgiven, precisely because the gift of forgiveness is given to us when we are the least deserving. 'While we were yet sinners, Christ died for us' (Rom 5:6).

When we begin to explore the specific character of Christian hope, dependent as it is upon the undeserved gift of our forgiveness, we discover an essentially receptive element within it. As Aquinas notes, the theological virtue of hope is related to fear, both because by fear we shrink from that which is evil (i.e. our sins) and because we stand in need of strengthening with respect to what is arduous. The cardinal virtue of fortitude as that which strengthens us to do what is difficult bears a certain similarity to the theological virtue of hope, yet the strength we receive in Christian hope does not arise within ourselves; it is received of God. The appropriate description given for this gift of strength in hope is that it is something we 'lean upon'.[12] Here hope speaks less to our difficulty in actively doing something than in bearing or suffering or enduring something.

This is borne out in the text from Romans. We rejoice, says Paul, in our hope, which comes to us as gift. But further, we rejoice in our sufferings. On the face of it, this is an extremely odd thing to say—unless of course one is a masochist.[13] Suffering is no fun, as Paul knew. Why, then, should we rejoice in it? We do so only when the sufferings come to us as gift. And we are only able to receive them as such when we hope. Christian hope puts a spin on our suffering, but it is a different spin than that for which it is commonly mistaken, namely the spin of explanation. Hope does not explain to us why we suffer; indeed, precisely because we hope, we recognize that our suffering lies beyond present explanation. Instead, hope places us squarely in a narrative in which our suffering can be endured and accordingly made part of our life. As we enter this narrative we are given the grace to see our suffering as leading somewhere; as a part of a journey that stretches before us toward a destination that includes sharing in the glory of God. Put abstractly this destination sounds fanciful. But Paul does not mean it abstractly. Our sufferings are not so much something that will someday (in the great beyond) bear fruit. Rather they are a form of our participation in Christ.[14]

Mention of Christ's suffering has a double meaning in this context, for we have come round to speak of our own suffering in the light of Christ's, all in a discussion which began with the sacrifice of Christ by which we are justified to God. In short, Christ's suffering brackets ours. Lest we forget the nature of this suffering, Paul reminds us in v. 7 that while suffering and death might be endured for a righteous man, Christ's suffering was endured for us, who are sinners. If, then, we participate in

Christ's suffering, we learn the endurance of Christ, which in turn can produce in us the character of Christ.

It is easy to associate endurance with passivity toward evil. Yet we must recall that evil, particularly evil as sin, is something we must learn to see. Conceived as misfortune, evil is rightly passively received, since nothing can be done about it. Raging against fortune, while possessed of a certain nobility, is deceived.[15] The reception of evil as the result of sin, on the other hand, is a positive act in the sense that another avenue is open, namely punishment, or even revenge. Fortune is impermeable to our retaliation; we cannot harm her. Persons who harm us, however, can be harmed in return; they can be made to pay the price of their injustice.

God's response to our sin was to forgive us, doing so by enduring suffering and death at the hands of those he came to redeem. We may be tempted by this description to suppose that our suffering in a similar way arises entirely out of injustice done to us. But of course the analogy does not hold, for, as Paul constantly reminds us, we are sinners. No doubt we do suffer injustices, and we are called to forgive them as Christ forgave us. We do so, however, not because we are righteous but because we are forgiven. More generally, however, whether deserved or undeserved, when drawn within the narrative of God's presence in human history in the Jews and in Jesus, our suffering produces an endurance which can turn our fate into calling. For in the narrative, we are given the means to turn our past, which is a history of sin, into love capable of being of service to the neighbour.

More often than not the term 'sin' is used to point to an act or set of acts that do not measure up. We need not call this a misuse of the term to offer another and deeper sense, namely that sin is a state in which we stand. Some call this state 'natural'; we hold, however, that it is better described as a history, one that holds us captive. The gift of hope which comes with the forgiveness offered in Christ's sacrifice frees us from this captivity, not so much extracting us from sin's history but by placing it in relation to a new future. As Paul elsewhere develops in Romans, this is a future life made possible by Christ's victory over sin and its principal effect, namely death. Indeed,

Christians can endure because through Christ they have been given power over death and all forms of victimization that trade on it. The ultimate power of Christ is the victory over death that makes possible the endurance of suffering; we can endure because we have confidence that though our enemies may kill us they cannot determine the meaning of our death. Christians have been given the power to overcome oppression, not by retaliation, but by the stalwart refusal to be defined as victims by the oppressor. We endure because no matter what may be done to us we know that those who threaten our death are powerless to determine the meaning of our lives by killing us. Likewise, our decisive service to our neighbour is to open to her a place where she is no longer a victim, of others or of herself. If we can relieve her suffering, we should, but more importantly we offer her the endurance to live with her suffering, now no longer meaningless, since it is carried by an eschatological hope that is confident in what it has already witnessed, namely Christ's victory over death.

Endurance, character, and hope

Endurance that allows us to rejoice in our suffering can never be described by Christians as an individual achievement, not only because it follows from a gift, but also because it is the endurance of a *whole people* committed to remembering the saints. From the saints we learn how to be steadfast in the face of adversity. By remembering them we become members of a community and history that gives us the power to prevail. Of course, the saints make no sense apart from the life and death of Jesus of Nazareth. The memory of them, therefore, derives its power from the memory of Him, whom we celebrate in a meal, a meal that offers us the opportunity to share together in His calling. The saints' faithfulness to this calling is concrete demonstration that by Jesus' resurrection a people is formed who can sustain the virtues necessary to remember His death.[16] As we sustain that memory, Christians receive the power to make our deaths our own by learning to endure.

Like suffering, endurance is not an end in itself, but produces character. On the other hand, neither is endurance merely the means to character. We do not suffer *so that* we may endure and we do not endure *so that* we may have character. Rather, in our suffering we learn endurance and in our endurance we learn of our character. For 'character' names the history we have been given through the endurance of our suffering. As such, our character is indeed an achievement, but one that comes as a gift.[17] Moreover, we attain character not by our constant effort to reach an ideal but by discovery, as we look back on our lives and, by God's forgiveness, claim them as our own. Character, in other words, names the continuity of our lives, the recognition of which is made possible by the retrospective affirmation that our lives are not just the sum of what we have done but rather are constituted by what God has done for us. In short, character is recognized in the discovery of those narratives that live through us, making us more than we could have hoped.

This is one reason Christian ethics is so at odds with other accounts of the moral life that assume ethical reflection and behaviour are primarily matters of prospective judgments about moral dilemmas. These accounts are built on rationalistic self-deceptions about the power each individual has autonomously to determine his or her 'choices'. In contrast Christian ethics, at least the kind we are willing to defend, is not concerned so much with decisions and choices but with the character of a person, who is as much the choices he did not make as those he made. While we are related to our choices, we are never entirely captured by them, since we know our character by discovery, as if a gift bestowed on us.

Finally, for Paul character (re)produces hope, this time a hope 'that does not disappoint' (v. 5). How are we to understand this relation? As we have been arguing, character is something we discover, a sort of epiphenomenon that arises with the endurance produced by suffering. But, as we have tried to make plain, this is not just any suffering nor any endurance. Rather, the character that is capable of producing hope is that formed within the story of God's redemption in the person of Jesus Christ. Put simply, the character of Christians is possible only if Jesus has in fact been raised from the dead.

To review the series of points we have been making in a slightly different vein, who we are and what we do has everything to do with what story we are in. This is so because stories form worlds. As Wittgenstein reminded us, the world of the happy person is not the same as the world of the unhappy. Or, as MacIntyre has argued regarding human action, we

> place the agent's intentions . . . in causal and temporal order with reference to their role in his or her history; and we also place them with reference to their role in the history of the setting or settings to which they belong. In doing this, in determining what causal efficacy the agent's intentions had in one or more directions, and how his short-term intentions succeeded or failed to be constitutive of long-term intentions, we ourselves write a further part of these histories. Narrative history of a certain kind turns out to be the basic and essential genre for the characterization of human actions.[18]

More than endurance or other virtues, character is a designation that marks the continuity present throughout the changes that constitute a complete human life. Remarkably, character in this context arises as we respond to our suffering by placing it within the narrative of God's redemptive activity for us. As we receive this narrative we discover it provides us the resources of character to make our past intelligible, including a past (and present) of suffering. Or, in other words, as we endure our suffering as the suffering of Christ we discover that God gives us a character capable of sustaining a hope that does not disappoint. Of course, we began this road with hope. The hope our journey has produced is not different from that with which it began except in this: as we began to hope, we could not anticipate where it would lead.

The character we have come to have through suffering and endurance is able to produce hope because by it we learn to inhabit the narrative of God's work in Jesus Christ and so to see all existence as trustworthy. Viewed otherwise, 'existence' does not warrant this assessment, but in the story that now shapes our character we grow to see all that is as a reflection of the glory of the God who made it. Hope, then, is not merely sustained but grows as we are taught to ask more and more of God's creation. In the language of the Scholastics, God's grace rewards itself by increasing in us the ability to enjoy God forever.

The Scholastics called this process 'merit,' perhaps an unfortunate choice of a word since it encourages the assumption that men and women might be able to place God's grace under necessity—i.e. by their efforts cause it to come about. Yet Aquinas insists that 'man is justified by faith not as though man, by believing, were to merit justification, but that he believes whilst he is being justified.'[19] We are ordained by God to an eternal life of friendship with God, not by our own strength but by the help of grace.'[20] In this sense, 'merit' but names the process by which God's grace becomes ours because of God's unwillingness to leave us alone. To return to the text in Romans, merit is nothing other than love 'poured into our hearts through the Holy Spirit'. Our hope begins in love as God justifies us even in out sin. Now, as the text demonstrates, hope also ends in love, one that is able to rejoice in all it has created. Love echoes love, yet it grows within us as we hope, suffer, and endure. Indeed, to deny love's growth is to deny the power of God's grace.

Like 'merit', one might prefer another term for the virtues we receive as we enter into the story of God's redemption in Christ than 'infused', the term Aquinas picks. Nonetheless, the point behind the designation is essential. The infused cardinal virtues—infused temperance, fortitude, justice, and prudence—come together with love, or Aquinas's theological virtue of *caritas*. While resembling the acquired cardinal virtues, they are different in species since they lead us to act in relation to our life with God.

Especially since, as we have been maintaining, the character produced by the endurance of suffering involves a certain unity of the self, it is important to consider a difficulty Aquinas's notion of infused virtue has occasioned. As Robert Sokolowski has put it, when the idea of infused virtues is introduced 'we seem to have not only a contrast between moral and theological virtues but also a contrast between two levels of moral virtues, the natural and the infused. In what

sense does one remain a single agent in such differences? . . .
[C]ould a person who is weak in self-control as regards natural virtue be, at the same time, temperate and courageous
through his infused virtue? Does he acquire such temperance
and courage simply by infusion, without actual performance?'[21] The difficulty is that we appear to be divided within
ourselves by grace. The set of infused virtues, as unified in
love, seems to threaten the intactness of the person of virtue
who has acquired his character by repeated acts.

One way to solve the apparent puzzle is to propose, as does
Sokolowski, that finally there is no difference between what
the good person and the Christian should do in the concrete—
i.e. to tell the truth, to be honest, to be temperate and courageous, to defend one's home and country.[22] This solution is
unsatisfactory, especially when we remember that the life of
virtue is a matter not only of action but also of passion and
perception. Indeed, Aquinas is rightly struggling with the fact
that the person whose life is lived in love and peace with God
simply does not live in the same world as the person whose is
not. As we might say, they inhabit different narrative contexts.
Translating Sokolowski's problem into this idiom, the problem
of the divided self arising from the distinction between the
infused and acquired virtues is a problem of divided narratives.[23]

This point opens a way to return to Barth and Meilaender,
and ultimately to sin. One need not deny that growth occurs to
affirm that, as wayfarers, our present selves are yet constituted
by two narratives. We are not yet what we will be; to suppose
that we are is a temptation not only to self-deception and
hubris, but also to a falsification of the world through which
we travel.

Yet the reality of this world (the world of sin) and the divid-
edness of our selves should strengthen rather than diminish
our resolve that this world should not determine our growth
in hope. No sin is more damning than to fail to hope in the
power of God's love to release us from our sin. Likewise, our
growth in grace is not a denial of our sinfulness but rather the
basis for our knowledge and acknowledgment of our sin.
Indeed, it is the common testimony of the saints that as they

draw closer to God, they are increasingly overwhelmed by the knowledge of their sin. As we have emphasized, without God's grace we cannot even know we are sinners. Precisely because God has invited us to be part of his kingdom, the truth of our sin can be known and confessed without that knowledge destroying us.

We can grow in Christian virtue, yet it is best to describe this as growth in grace, whose hallmark is forgiveness. (That is, if we do not forgive—and perhaps even more—if we refuse to be forgiven, we grow neither in virtue nor in grace.) We forgive not as a people who by their own perfection can do so gratuitously, but rather as those who have themselves been forgiven. The test of that forgiveness is, in fact, our own willingness to receive it from others, a test, as we have argued before, that most 'men of virtue' (such as Aristotle's) would fail, with clear and haughty intent. Our acceptance of forgiveness is the means by which our souls are expanded so that we can hope. Through hope we learn to endure suffering, confident that God has given us the character faithfully to inhabit the story of the redemption of all creation, of which we are part. While we inevitably live divided lives, we can grow in the unity of the story so that our virtues might finally be unified. That is why all virtues for Christians cannot but be hopeful ones.[24]

Endnotes

[1] For a full-blown attempt to show how the Bible can be explicated in terms of the virtues, see Benjamin Farley, *In Praise of Virtue: An Explication of the Biblical Virtues in a christian context* (Grand Rapids: Eerdmans, 1995).

[2] Karl Barth, *Church Dogmatics*, II/2 (Edinburgh: T. and T. Clark, 1957), pp. 644–45.

[3] Ibid., p. 612.

[4] Gilbert Meilaender, *The Limits of Love: Some Theological Explorations* (University Park: Pennsylvania State University Press, 1987), p. 35. The earlier and more complete version can be found in "The Place of Ethics in the Theological Task," *Currents in Theology and Mission* 6 (1979): 199.

[5] Ibid., pp. 35 and 199 respectively.

[6] Meilaender, *The Limits of Love*, p. 36. For an account of justification we unreservedly endorse see David Yeago, "The Promise of God and the Desires of Our Hearts: Prolegomena to a Lutheran Retrieval of Classical Spiritual Theology," *Lutheran Forum* 30, 2 (May 1996), pp. 21-30. Yeago puts it right when he observes, "The *content* of the gospel is *not* justification, *not* forgiveness, not acceptance; the content of the gospel, what it talks about, what it promises, is Jesus Christ" (27). See also, David Yeago, "Gnosticism, Antinomianism, and Reformation Theology: Reflections on the Costs of a Construal," *Pro Ecclesia* 2, 1 (winter 1993), pp.37–49.

[7] Edmund Pincoffs, *Quandries and Virtues: Against Reductionism in Ethics*, p. 162.

[8] Alasdair MacIntyre, *After Virtue*, pp. 204–25. In *Whose Justice? Which Rationality?* MacIntyre argues not only that the virtues are tradition-specific but so also are the desires. "We are apt to suppose under the influence of this type of modern view that desires are psychologically basic items, largely, even if not entirely, invariant in their function between cultures. This is a mistake. The role and function of desires in the self-understanding of human beings vary from culture to culture with the way in which their projects and aspirations, expressions of need and claims upon others, are organized and articulated in the public social world" (p. 21). If MacIntyre is right about this, and we believe he is, any attempt to construe the virtues in terms of the formation of "invariant" desires and/or passions is rendered problematic. For a somewhat different perspective see Paul Lewis, "Rethinking Emotion and the Moral Life in Light of Thomas Aquinas and Jonathan Edwards" (Ph.D. diss., Duke University, 1991).

[9] J. Christiaan Beker, *Paul's Apocalyptic Gospel: The Coming Triumph of God* (Philadelphia: Fortress Press, 1982), p. 30.

[10] Robert Roberts, "Virtue and Rules," *Philosophy and Phenomenological Research* 5, 2 (1991): 325 ff.

[11] Robert Roberts, "Therapies and the Grammar of a Virtue," in *The Grammar of the Heart: New Essays in Moral Philosophy and Theology*, ed. Richard H. Bell (San Francisco: Harper and Row, 1988), pp. 14–15.

[12] Thomas Aquinas, *ST* II–II, 17, 1.

[13] Masochism is a troubling concept, as we by no means wish to endorse the presumption that the acceptance of suffering is pathological, although in certain instances it may be. The therapeutic context which produces a notion like masochism often presumes accounts of human existence that entail that all suffering is "bad."

14 For more extended reflection on those matters see Hauerwas's *Naming the Silences: God, Medicine and the Problem of Evil* (Grand Rapids: Eerdmans, 1990). This does not mean that suffering is closer to the absurd, but rather that bearing the 'pointlessness' of some kinds of suffering becomes part of our service to God.

15 Earlier in chapter 5 of *Christians Among the Virtues* we claimed that this is what Christians do—they rage against fortune. But of course there, as here, the deeper question involves whether Christians can use the language of fortune at all. And clearly they cannot use it indiscriminately, since they acknowledge God is both the creator and sustenance of the universe. When Christians 'rage against fortune' they do so less against fortune herself (as does, say, Camus's Dr. Rieux in *The Plague*), more so against the hegemony of 'fortune' as the last word.

16 For a powerful account of sainthood that develops this theme see David Matzko, *Hazarding Theology: Theological Descriptions and Particular Lives* (Ph.D. diss., Duke University, 1992).

17 We are indebted to Alasdair MacIntyre for this way of putting the point. For a more developed account of character see Hauerwas, *Character and the Christian Life: A Study in Theological Ethics* (Notre Dame: University of Notre Dame Press, 1994).

18 *After Virtue*, p. 208.

19 *ST* I–II, 114, 6.

20 Ibid., I–II, 114, 2.

21 Robert Sokolowski, *The God of Faith and Reason* (Notre Dame: University of Notre Dame Press, 1982), p. 78.

22 Ibid., p. 82.

23 Aquinas makes the interesting point that the infused moral virtues may encounter difficulty in acting as they contend with dispositions remaining from previous acts. Since the acquired virtues result from previous acts, they are not so likely to have this difficulty. The implication seems to be that we are held back from living as the infused virtues direct us precisely because we have another history which yet holds us in its sway. *ST* I–II, 65, 3.

24 For the development of the idea that the Christian moral life involves finding our life as part of God's life see Hauerwas's *The Peaceable Kingdom: A Primer in Christian Ethics* (Notre Dame: University of Notre Dame Press, 1983). See L. Gregory Jones, *Embodying Forgiveness: A Theological Analysis* (Grand Rapids: Eerdemans, 1995) for a compelling account of forgiveness as a practice.

Chapter 6

The Servant Community

Stanley Hauerwas

Social ethics and qualified ethics

Christian ethics would be unintelligible if it did not presuppose the existence and recognizability of communities and corresponding institutions capable of carrying the story of God. The most general name we give that community is church, but there are other names for it in the history of Christianity. It is 'the way', the body of Christ, people of God, and a plethora of images that denote the social reality of being Christian and what it means to be a distinctive people formed by the narrative of God. We should remember that the name 'church' is no less an image than 'people of God'. In fact, one of the issues in theology is which images of the church are primary or controlling for the others.

Thus, the claim that there is no ethic without a qualifier itself implies that a Christian ethic is always a *social* ethic. Indeed, the notion that one can distinguish between personal and social ethics distorts the nature of Christian convictions, for Christians refuse to admit that 'personal' morality is less a community concern than questions of justice, and so on. 'Personal' issues may, of course, present different kinds of concern to the community from those of justice, but they are no less social for being personal.

At a general level there is much to be said for the contention that every ethic is a social ethic. The self is fundamentally social. We are not individuals who come into contact with others and then decide our various levels of social involvement. Our individuality is possible only because we are first of all social beings. I know who I am only in relation to others, and, indeed, who I am is a relation with others. The 'self' names not a thing, but a relation.[1]

But the claim that Christian ethic is a social ethic is even stronger than those now commonplace observations about the self's sociality. We have seen that the content of Christian ethics involves claims about a kingdom. Therefore, the first words about the Christian life are about a life together, not about the individual. This kingdom sets the standard for the life of the church, but the life of the kingdom is broader than that of the church. For the church does not possess Christ; his presence is not confined to the church. Rather, it is in the church that we learn to recognize Christ's presence outside the church.

The church is not the kingdom but the foretaste of the kingdom. In the church the narrative of God is lived in a way that makes the kingdom visible. The church must be the clear manifestation of a people who have learned to be at peace with themselves, one another, the stranger, and of course, most of all, God. There can be no sanctification of individuals without a sanctified people. Like apprentices who learn their crafts by working alongside the master-craftsman, we Christians need exemplars or saints whose lives embody the kingdom way. If we lack such exemplars, the church cannot exist as a people who are pledged to be different from the world.

Therefore we see that contained in the claim that there is no ethic without a qualifier—a claim that at the beginning seemed to be primarily a methodological one—is a strong substantive assumption about the status and necessity of the church as the locus for Christian ethical reflection. It is from the church that Christian ethics draws its ethical substance and it is to the church that Christian ethical reflection is first addressed. Christian ethics is not written for everyone, but for those people who have been formed by the God of Abraham, Isaac, Jacob, and Jesus, since Christian ethics presupposes a sanctified people wanting to live more faithful to God's story, and thus it cannot be a minimalistic ethic for everyone.

The story of God as told through the experience of Israel and the church cannot be abstracted from those communities engaged in the telling and the hearing. As a story it cannot exist without a community existing across time, for it requires telling and remembering. God has entrusted his presence to a historic and contingent community that must be renewed generation after generation. The story is not merely told but embodied in a people's habits that form and are formed in worship, governance, and morality.

Therefore the existence of Israel and the church is not accidentally related to the story but is necessary for our knowledge of God. You cannot tell the story of God without including within it the story of Israel and the church. Thus we affirm as part of the creed that we believe in the One Holy Catholic and Apostolic Church. We believe in the church in the sense that we know that it is not finally our creation, but exists only by God's calling of people. Moreover, it is only through such a people that the world can know that our God is one who wills nothing else than our good. To be sure, the church is often unfaithful, but God refuses to let that unfaithfulness be the last word. God creates and sustains a peaceable people in the world, generation after generation.

In a sense, the place of the Bible can be misleading in this aspect, because it may appear that Scripture conveys the story independently of the existence of a historic people. You do not need an intergenerational community. All you need is the story told rightly in a book. But without a community of expounders, interpreters, and hearers, the Bible is a dead book.

Of course, Scripture stands over the community exerting a critical function, but that it does so is an aspect of the community's self-understanding. Scripture is the means the church uses to constantly test its memory. That is why it can never be content with using just one part of Scripture, but must struggle day in and day out with the full text. For the story the church must tell as well as embody is a many-sided tale that constantly calls us from complacency and conventions. Scripture has authority in the church; Scripture sets the agenda and boundaries for a truthful conversation. Those with true authority, then, are those who would serve by helping the church better hear and correspond to the stories of God as we find them in Scripture. Thus we are told, 'A dispute also arose among them, which of them was to be regarded as the greatest. And he said to them, "The kings of the Gentiles exercise lordship over them; and those in authority over them are called benefactors. But not so with you; rather let the greatest among you become as the youngest, and the leader as one who serves. For which is the greater, one who sits at table, or one who serves? Is it not the one who sits at the table? But I am among you as one who serves"' (Luke 22:24–27).

The church is a social ethic

But what does all this have to do with social ethics? What does this emphasis on the church tell us about what we should be doing in third-world countries? Or what we Christians ought to be doing in this country to ensure social justice? What should be our response to war? These are the kinds of questions that are most often thought to constitute social ethics, not questions about the place of Scripture in the church's life.

Furthermore, once we accept the neutrality of these questions for social ethics we feel the pull of natural law as the essential feature of Christian ethics. For to accomplish justice, to work for a more nearly free and equitable social order requires cooperation with non-Christians. If Christian social ethics depends on sources peculiar to Christians, then it seems that the prospects for achieving a more just society will be weakened. Even worse, it presents the specter of Christians seeking to form Christian states or societies (and we are well versed in the real and supposed histories of repression and coercion in such efforts). But surely in matters of social ethics there must be moral generalities anchored in our social nature that provide the basis for common moral commitment and action. Surely in social ethics we should downplay the distinctively Christian and emphasize that we are all people of good will as we seek to work for a more peaceable and just world for everyone.

Yet that is exactly what I am suggesting we should *not* do. I am challenging the very idea that the primary goal of

Christian social ethics should be an attempt to make the world more peaceable or just. Rather, *the first social ethical task of the church is to be the church—the servant community*. Such a claim may well sound self-serving until we remember that what makes the church the church is its faithful manifestation of the peaceable kingdom in the world. *As such, the church does not have a social ethic; the church is a social ethic.*

The church is where the stories of Israel and Jesus are told, enacted, and heard. As a Christian people, there is literally nothing more important we can do. But the telling of that story requires that we be a particular kind of people if we and the world are to hear the story truthfully. That means that the church must never cease from being a community of peace and truth in a world of mendacity and fear. The church does not let the world set its agenda about what constitutes a 'social ethic', but a church of peace and justice must set its own agenda. It does this first by having the patience amid the injustice and violence of this world to care for the widow, the poor, and the orphan. Such care, from the world's perspective, may seem to contribute little to the cause of justice, yet it is our conviction that unless we take the time for such care neither we nor the world can know what justice looks like.

By being that kind of community we see that the church helps the world understand what it means to be the world. The world is God's world, God's good creation, which is all the more distorted by sin because it still is bounded by God's goodness. For the church to be the church it must show what the world is meant to be as God's good creation. For the world has no way of knowing it is the world without the church pointing to the reality of God's kingdom. How could the world ever recognize the arbitrariness of the divisions between people if it did not have a contrasting model in the unity of the church? Only against the church's universality can the world have the means to recognize the arbitrariness of the national and racial divisions resulting in violence and war.

The scandal of the disunity of the church is even more painful when we recognize this social task. For all too often it appears that we who have been called to be the foretaste of the peaceable kingdom fail to maintain unity among ourselves. As a result we abandon the world to its own devices. The divisions I speak of in the church are not only those based on doctrine, history, or practices, important though they are. The deepest and most painful divisions afflicting the church in America are those based on class, race, and nationality that we have sinfully accepted as written into the nature of things.

We must remember that the 'world' as that opposed to God is not an ontological designation. Thus, 'world' is not inherently sinful; rather, its sinful character comes from its own free will. The only difference between church and world is the difference between agents. As Yoder suggests, the distinction between church and world is not between realms of reality, between orders of creation and redemption, between nature and supernature, but 'rather between the basic personal postures of men and women, some of whom confess and others of whom do not confess that Jesus is Lord. The distinction between church and the world is not something that God has imposed upon the world by a prior metaphysical definition, nor is it only something which timid or pharisaical Christians have built up around themselves. It is all of that in creation that has taken the freedom not yet to believe.'[2]

In this respect, moreover, it is particularly important to remember that the world consists of those, including ourselves, who have chosen not to make the story of God their story. The world in us refuses to affirm that this is God's world and that, as loving Lord, God's care for creation is greater than our illusion of control. The world is those aspects of our individual and social lives where we live untruthfully by continuing to rely on violence to bring order.

Church and world are thus relational concepts: neither is intelligible without the other. They are companions on a journey that makes it impossible for one to survive without the other, though each constantly seeks to do so. They are thus more often enemies than friends, an enmity tragically arising from the church's attempt to deny its calling and service to the world—dismissing the world as irredeemable or transforming its own servant status into a trumphalist subordination of the world. But God has in fact redeemed the world, even if the world refuses to the hopelessness deriving from its rejection of

God, but must be a people with a hope sufficiently fervent to sustain the world as well as itself.

As Christians we will at times find that people who are not Christians manifest God's peace better than we ourselves. It is to be hoped that such people may provide the conditions for our ability to cooperate with others for securing justice in the world. Such cooperation, however, is not based on a 'natural law' legitimation of a generally shared 'natural morality'. Rather, it is a testimony to the fact that God's kingdom is wide indeed. As the church we have no right to determine the boundaries of God's kingdom, for it is our happy task to acknowledge God's power to make his kingdom present in the most surprising places and ways.

Thus the church serves the world by giving the world the means to see itself truthfully. *The first question we must ask is not 'What should we do?' but 'What is going on?'*[3] Our task as church is the demanding one of trying to understand rightly the world as world, to face realistically what the world is with its madness and irrationality.

Therefore, calling for the church to be the church is not a formula for a withdrawal ethic, nor is it a self-righteous attempt to flee from the world's problems. Rather, it is a call for the church to be a community that tries to develop the resources to stand within the world witnessing to the peaceable kingdom. The gospel is political. Christians are engaged in politics, a politics of the kingdom. Such a politics reveals the insufficiency of all politics based on coercion and falsehood, and it finds the true source of power in servanthood rather than domination.

This is not to imply that the church is any less a human community than other forms of human association. As with other institutions, the church draws on and requires patterns of authority that derive from human needs for status, belonging, and direction. The question is not whether the church is a natural institution, as it surely is, but how it shapes that 'nature' in accordance with its fundamental convictions.[4] 'Nature' provides the context for community but does not determine its character.

While the church clearly is a polity, it is a polity *unlike* any other insofar as it is formed by a people who have no reason to fear the truth. They seek to exist in the world without resorting to coercion to maintain their presence. Their ability to sustain this presence depends to a large extent on their willingness to move—they must be 'a moveable feast'. For it is certain that much of the world is bound to hate them for truthfully naming the world. They cannot and should not wish to provoke the world's violence, but if it comes they must resist even if that resistance requires them to leave one place for another. For as Christians we are at home in no nation. Our true home is the church itself, where we find those who, like us, have been formed by a saviour who was necessarily always on the move.

A community of virtues

For the church to *be* rather than to *have* a social ethic requires a certain kind of people to sustain it as an institution across time. They must be a people of virtue—specifically, the virtues necessary for remembering and telling the story of a crucified saviour. They must be capable of being peaceable among themselves and with the world, so that the world sees what it means to hope for God's kingdom. In such a community, we are not free to do whatever we will but are called to develop our particular gifts to serve the community of faith.

James Gustafson has right argued that all human communities require virtues in order to be sustained. People in a community must learn to trust one another as well as trust the community itself.[5] Moreover, all communities require a sense of hope in the future and they witness so the necessity of love for sustaining relationships. Therefore, there is a profound sense in which the traditional 'theological virtues' of faith, hope, and love are 'natural.' As much as any institution the church is sustained by these 'natural virtues'. However, the kind of faith, hope, and love that must be displayed among Christians derives from the tradition that molds their community. Christians are the community of a new age that must continue so exist in the old age (2 Cor 5:16–17). As a people 'on a way', they make certain virtues central.

Patience, for example, is a crucial virtue for Christians seeking to live amid this violent world as a peaceable people. Though we know that the kingdom has come in Jesus and is present in the breaking of bread, it is still to come. Sustained by the kingdom's having come and fueled by its presence, we hope all the more for its complete fulfillment, but this hope must be schooled by a patience, lest it turns into fanaticism or cynicism.

The church must learn time and time again that its task is not to *make* the world the kingdom, but to be faithful to the kingdom by showing to the world a community of peace. Thus we are required to be patient and never lose hope. But hope in what? Specifically, hope in the God who has promised that faithfulness to the kingdom will be of use in God's care for the world. Thus our ultimate hope is not in this world, or in humankind's goodness, or in some sense that everything always works out for the best, but in God and God's faithful caring for the world.

Especially with regard to questions of justice we see the importance of the interrelationship of hope and patience. For it is a matter of justice that those who are hungry should be fed, that those who are abandoned should be cared for, that those who have been oppressed and maltreated should be freed and respected. Yet we know that while justice demands all these things, we live in a world where injustice seems to dominate. For in this world, the hungry are fed, the abandoned cared for, the oppressed freed, it seems, only if it can be done without anyone's feeling the pinch.

When a people who have been trained to hunger and thirst for righteousness are confronted with this reality, especially if they are no longer poor, they may be sorely tempted to turn to violence. How can we continue to face the poor without allowing the possibility of coercion to see that at least minimal justice is done? For there is no question that violence 'works' in some circumstances to relieve the burden of the poor. Indeed, one of their primary weapons is violence, since they are a people with nothing to lose—and such people are the most threatening of all for those of us who have something to lose. Most of us would rather bargain away some of our possessions than have to deal with the threat of violence from those who have so little.

But the justice that the church seeks cannot be derived from envy or fear. Rather, we seek a justice that comes from a people who know their possessions are a gift in the first place. Therefore, Christians cannot support 'justice' coming from the barrel of a gun, and we must be suspicious of that 'justice' that relies on manipulation of our less than worthy motives. For God does not rule creation through coercion, but through a cross. As Christians, therefore, we seek not so much to be effective as to be faithful. We cannot seek 'results' that require us to employ unjust means. Christians have rightly felt much in accord with those, such as Kant, who argue that there are some things we cannot do, no matter what good might accrue.

We must be a people who have learned to be patient in the face of injustice. But it may be objected: Surely that is too easily said if you are not the ones who are suffering from injustice. Precisely, but that does not mean that we ought to legitimize the use of force to overcome injustice. Such legitimation often comes from the attempt to have justice without risking the self, as when we ask the 'state' or the 'revolution' to see that justice is done, but in a manner that does not significantly affect our own material position. If we are to be a hopeful and patient people in a world of injustice, however, we cannot merely identify with the 'cause' of the poor; we must become poor and powerless.

Too often, ideals and strategies for 'social justice' are but formulas that attempt to make the poor and oppressed better off without requiring anything of us. Thus when we read that the poor, the merciful, the peacemakers, the meek, the persecuted, the pure in heart are blessed, we may well presume those descriptions of 'blessedness' apply to anyone who would be a follower of Jesus. But the fundamental question we must address to ourselves as Christians is: How is it that we who are Christians are so rich? Furthermore, has our being rich led us to misread the gospel as essentially an apolitical account of individual salvation, rather than the good news of the creation of a new community of peace and justice formed by a hope that God's kingdom has and will prevail?

Moreover, the virtues of patience and hope are necessary to be a people who must learn to 'live out of control'. While not all senses of 'living out of control' are relevant for determining the character of the Christian community, 'living out of control' is important in that it suggests that Christians base their lives on the knowledge that God has redeemed his creation through the work of Jesus of Nazareth. We thus live out of control in the sense that we must assume God will use our faithfulness to make his kingdom a reality in the world.

To live out of control, however, does not mean that we do not plan and/or seek to find the means to promote justice in the world, but that such planning is not done under the illusion of omnipotence. We can take the risk of planning that does not make effectiveness our primary goal, but faithfulness to God's kingdom. To plan in such a manner involves breaking the cycle of self-deception that leads to the belief that justice can be achieved only through a power and violence that seeks to assure its efficacy.

Ironically, those who are most controlled are those who (mistakenly) assume that they are in control. Wealth is particularly insidious in giving its bearers the illusion of independence, separateness, and 'being in control'. But all of us in one way or another willingly submit to the illusion that we can rid our world of chance and surprise. Yet when we try to live securely rather than well, our world begins to shrink. For example, ironically, people in power often become controlled by their subordinates, who tell them only what they want to hear. They thus lose the capacity to deal with the unexpected except by ignoring it, suppressing it, or eliminating it. Such people do not yet understand that the trick to living well is learning to see the unexpected as our greatest resource.

To live out of control, then, is to renounce the illusion that our task as Christians is to make history come out right.[6] We do not write social ethics from the perspective of those who would claim to be in control and 'in power.' Rather, we believe that a more truthful account of what is really going on in the world comes from those who are 'out of control'. For those who are without control have fewer illusions about what makes this world secure or safe, and they inherently distrust those who say they are going to help through power and violence. The apropos perspective when writing Christian social ethics, therefore, is not that of the secretary of state or the president, but the perspective of those who are subject to such people.

The task of the Christian people is not to seek to control history, but to be faithful to the mode of life of the peaceable kingdom. Such a people can never lose hope in the reality of that kingdom, but they must surely also learn to be patient. For they must often endure injustice that might appear to be quickly eliminated through violence. Moreover, they can never acquiesce in the injustice, for to do so would only leave the neighbour to his or her own devices. Those who are violent, who are our neighbours, must be resisted, but resisted on *our* terms, because not to resist is to abandon them to sin and injustice.

Such resistance may appear to the world as foolish and ineffective for it may involve something so small as refusing to pay a telephone tax to support a war, but that does not mean that it is not resistance. Such resistance at least makes clear that Christian social witness can never take place in a manner than excludes the possibility of miracles, or surprises, of the unexpected. As Yoder frankly states, 'Christian ethics calls for behaviour which is impossible except by the miracle of the Holy Spirit.'[7] But that is the way it must be for a people who believe their very existence is nothing less than a continuing miracle.

The 'marks' of the church

For miracles happen here and there—indeed, we believe the very existence of the church to be a miracle. However, to speak of the church as a continuing miracle simply does not sound like any church we know or experience. The church is not just a 'community' but an institution that has budgets, buildings, parking lots, potluck dinners, heated debates about who should be the next pastor, and so on. What do these matters pertaining to the institutional form of the church have to do with the church as the miracle of God's continuing presence in our midst?

The people of God are no less an empirical reality than the crucifixion of Christ. The church is as real as his cross. There is no 'ideal church', no 'invisible church', no 'mystically existing universal church' more real than the concrete church with parking lots and potluck dinners. It is the church of parking lots and potluck dinners that comprises the sanctified ones formed by and forming the continuing story of Jesus Christ in the world. There are certainly differences in the church that may even cause separation, but that too is part of what it means to call the church an extended argument over time about the significance of that story and how best to understand it. In this vein, this is a reason why the church should learn to value her heretics, since the church also learns what it believes by learning what it does not believe.

No conversation over differences is more important than that between Israel and the church. For it is from Israel that we learn of the God who is present to us in the life, cross, and resurrection of Jesus. It is from Israel's continuing willingness to wait for the Messiah that we learn better how we much wait between the times. The church and Israel are two people walking in the path provided by God; they cannot walk independently of one another, for if they do they both risk becoming lost.[8]

The church, therefore, is not some ideal of community but a particular people who, like Israel, must find the way to sustain their existence generation after generation. Indeed, there are clear 'marks' through which we know that the church is church. These marks do not guarantee the existence of the church, but are the means God has given us to help us along the way. Thus the church is known where the sacraments are celebrated, the word is preached, and upright lives are encouraged and lived. Some churches emphasize one of these 'marks' more than others, but that does not mean that they are deficient in some decisive manner. What is important is that these 'marks' are exhibited by Christians everywhere, not that each particular body of Christians does all of these things.

In the sacraments we enact the story of Jesus and in so doing form a community in his image. We could not be the church without them. For the story of Jesus is not simply one that is told; it must be enacted. The sacraments are means crucial to shaping and preparing us to tell and hear that story. Thus baptism is the rite of initiation necessary for us to become part of Jesus' death and resurrection. Through baptism we do not simply learn the story, but *we become part of that story.* The eucharist is the eschatological meal of God's continuing presence that makes possible a peaceable people. At that meal we become part of Christ's kingdom, as we learn there that death could not contain him. His presence, his peace is a living reality in the world. As we partake we become part of his sacrifice, God's sacrifice, so that the world might be saved from sin and death.

These rites, baptism and eucharist, are not just 'religious things' that Christian people do. They are the essential rituals of our politics. Through them we enact who we are. These liturgies do not motivate us for effective social work; rather, these liturgies *are* our effective social work. For if the church *is* rather than *has* a social ethic, these actions are our most important social witness. In baptism and eucharist we see most clearly the marks of God's kingdom in the world. They see our standard, as we try to bring every aspect of our lives under their sway.[9]

Baptism and eucharist are also our most fervent prayers and set the standard for all of our other prayers. For prayer is not our pleading to an unmoveable or unsympathetic but all-powerful God. Through these and other prayers, we learn to make ourselves open to God's presence. Prayer is the way we let God loose in the world.[10] As such, prayer is a dangerous activity, for God's presence is not easily controlled. God is a wild presence calling us to ways of life we had not previously imagined possible. Through baptism and the eucharist Christian people open themselves to that wildness. It is no wonder that throughout history various rulers and powers have sought to prevent Christians from praying, since there is no more powerful challenge to their power.

In addition to praying, Christians also preach. There is no story without witness, and it is through the preaching of God's good news and our willingness to hear it that we become a people of witness. Preaching involves not only 'telling', but also hearing. Just as great art creates an audience capable of hearing or seeing in new ways, so the church's preaching creates an audience capable of being challenged in new ways by the story of Jesus and his kingdom.

Our preaching, however, cannot be confined to ourselves, because we become witnesses to those who do not share our story. In fact, the very content of that story requires us to address the stranger. God had promised us that where the word is rightly preached (and heard), it will be fruitful. Through the witnessing to the story of Jesus Christ generation after generation, God will create a people capable of carrying into the world the story of Jesus and his kingdom.

Therefore, just as baptism and the eucharist are essential to the church's social ethic, so is our preaching. Our obligation to witness arises from the conviction that there are no people beyond the power of God's word. Christians know no 'barbarians' but only strangers whom we hope to make our friends. We extend hospitality to God's kingdom by inviting the stranger to share our story. Of course, we know that the stranger does not come to us as a cipher, but also has a story to tell us. Through the stranger's reception of the story of Jesus (which may often take the form of rejection), we too learn more fully to hear the story of God. Without the constant challenge of the stranger—who often, interestingly enough, is but one side of ourselves—we are tempted to so domesticate Jesus' story that we lose the power of it.

But neither the marks of sacraments nor preaching would be sufficient if the church was not also called to be a holy people—that is, a people capable of maintaining a life of charity, hospitality, and justice. Thus the church must vigorously attend to mutual upbuilding and correction. We seek out the other because it is from the other than we learn how well or how poorly we have made the story of Jesus our story. For the church is finally known by the character of the people who constitute it, and if we lack that character, the world rightly draws the conclusion that the God we worship is in fact a false God.

It would be a mistake, moreover, to separate this emphasis on being a holy people from that of being a sacramental people. For I think it is not accidental that one of the classical Eucharistic texts appears in the context of moral exhortation. In 1 Corinthians 11:17–26 Paul says:

> But in the following instructions I do not commend you, because when you come together it is not for the better but for the worse. For in the first place, when you assemble as a church, I hear that there are divisions among you; and I partly believe it, for there must be factions among you in order that those who are genuine among you may be recognized. When you meet together, it is not the Lord's supper that you eat. For in eating, each one goes ahead with his own meal, and one is hungry and another is drunk. What! Do you not have houses to eat and drink in? Or do you despise the church of God and humiliate those who have nothing? What shall I say to you? Shall I commend you in this? No, I will not. For I received from the Lord what I also delivered to you: that the Lord Jesus on the night when he was betrayed took bread, and when he had given thanks, he broke it, and said, 'This is my body which is for you. Do this in remembrance of me.' In the same way also he took the cup, after supper, saying, 'This cup is the new covenant in my blood. Do this, as often as you drink it, in remembrance of me.' For as often as you eat this bread and drink the cup, you proclaim the Lord's death until he comes.

Our eating with our Lord is not different from our learning to be his disciples, his holy people. The kind of holiness that marks the church, however, is not that of moral perfection, but the holiness of a people who have learned not to fear one another and thus are capable of love. We do not just go ahead with our meals or our lives, but we wait for each other, so we may learn to live in the presence of others without fear and envy. We thus become a perfect people through the meal we share with our Lord. We learn that forgiveness of the enemy, even when the enemy is ourselves, is the way God would have his kingdom accomplished.

In his illuminating book about his missionary work with the Masai, Vincent Donovan powerfully illustrates the inherent relation between our holiness as a people and our eucharistic celebrations. One of the most significant gestures for the Masai is to offer one another a handful of grass as a sign of peace, happiness, and well-being. During arguments, for example, a tuft of grass might be offered by one Masai to another as an assurance that no violence would erupt because of this argument. 'No Masai would violate that sacred sign of peace offered, because it was not only a sign of peace; it was peace.'[11]

Donovan describes how the beginning of a Mass among the Masai would involve the whole village, as every activity of the village, from praying for the sick to dancing, would become a natural part of the Mass. Yet he says he never knew if the eucharist would emerge from all this. The leaders of the village were the ones to decide yes or no. 'If there had been selfishness and forgetfulness and hatefulness and lack of forgiveness in the work that had been done, in the life that had been led here, let them not make a sacrilege out of it by calling it the body of Christ. And the leaders did decide occasionally that, despite the prayers and readings and discussions, if the grass had stopped—if someone, or some group, in the village had refused to accept the grass as the sign of peace of Christ—there would be no eucharist at this time.'[12]

The social ethics of the church

It may be objected that all this still remains very abstract. Even if it is true that the church itself is a social ethic, surely it must also have a social ethic that reaches out in strategic terms in the societies in which it finds itself. That is certainly the case, but a social ethic in this latter sense cannot be done in the abstract. For there is no universal social strategy of the church that applies equally to diverse social circumstances. Indeed, different circumstances and social contexts require different responses and strategies. For example, the church's stance in the context of totalitarian governments is obviously different from its stance in liberal democratic regimes.

This does not mean the church must have a particular theory of government that can help it to understand the different ways it responds to totalitarian regimes as opposed to the more liberal democratic ones. The contemporary church has often assumed that it favours 'democratic' societies because such societies have institutionalized the freedom of religion through legal recognition of the freedom of conscience. But the assumption that democracies are intrinsically more just because they provide more freedom than other kinds of societies is misleading at best. For 'freedom' often functions as an abstraction that serves merely to direct our attention away from faithfully serving as the church. With regard to freedom, the crucial questions are 'What kind of freedom?' and 'How do we plan to use it?'

Yet it may be suggested that even if there is no one theory of government intrinsic to the church's self-understanding, surely there are some values which may have diverse institutional forms, that the church has a stake in promoting. For example, Enda McDonagh speaks of 'kingdom values', such as freedom, inviolability of the person, and equality, as necessary correlatives of the Christian commitment. Indeed, the church's promotion of these values in wider society is entailed by the Christian duty to promote more nearly just social orders. Christians, according to McDonagh, support these 'values' as intrinsic to the kingdom, but they are not peculiar to Christians *per se*. Rather, the pursuit of justice 'not only allows for cooperation with the non-believer, it opens up the non-believer and believer to an awareness of the human, the mystery of the human . . . In this way the discernment and promotion of social justice provides a pedagogy of the faith, a learning experience that has the capacity, under the attracting power of self-giving and revealing God whom we are encountering in the neighbour, to be transcended into explicit recognition of God, into faith. Not only does faith demand social justice, social justice finally demands faith—for the believer, increases in faith.'[13]

It is extremely interesting to compare McDonagh's position in this respect with that of Yoder. For Yoder says:

> The ultimate and most profound reason to consider Christ—rather than democracy or justice, or equality of liberty—as the hope of the world, is not the negative observation, clear enough already, that hopes of this kind generally remain incomplete

and disappointing, or that they can lead those who trust them to pride or brutality. The fundamental limitation of these hopes is found in the fact that in their search for power and in the urgency with which they seek to guarantee justice they are still not powerful enough. They locate the greatest need of man in the wrong place . . . Those for whom Jesus Christ is the hope of the world will for this reason not measure their contemporary social involvement by its efficacy for tomorrow nor by its success in providing work, or freedom, or food, or in building new social structures, but by identifying with the Lord in whom they have placed their trust.[14]

Yoder is not objecting to McDonagh's concern for justice, nor does he wish to deny that God requires that we seek justice for all people. Rather, he notices that 'justice' can mean—and thus require—many different things, and not all are equally amenable to Jesus' proclamation of the kingdom. Furthermore, once 'justice' is made a criterion of Christian social strategy, it can too easily take on a meaning and life of its own that is not informed by fundamental Christian convictions. For example, the appeal to 'justice' can and has been used to justify the Christian's resort to violence to secure a more 'relative justice.' But is this the justice we are to seek as Christians?

Put differently, the problem with identifying, or at least closely associating, the meaning of the gospel with the pursuit of 'kingdom values' such as justice, freedom, and equality is that such values lack the specificity and concreteness of the kingdom as found in Jesus' life and death. It is not sufficient to interpret, as McDonagh does, the eschatological nature of freedom and equality by noting that they are ideals never fully realized.[15] The problem is not that the kingdom brought by Christ is too idealistic to be realized. The problem is just the opposite. The kingdom present in Jesus Christ is the ultimate realism that rightly calls into question vague, secular ideals of freedom, equality, and peace. In other words, we do not learn about the demands of the kingdom by learning about freedom and equality; rather, we must first experience the kingdom if we are even to know what kind of freedom and what kind of equality we should desire. Christian freedom lies in service, and Christian equality is equality before God, and neither can be achieved through the coercive efforts of liberal idealists who would transform the world into their image.

Put in terms that have now become familiar, freedom and equality are not self-interpreting, but require a tradition to give them specificity and content. For example, it is a truism of political theory that freedom of the individual and a more egalitarian society are not consistent ideals—that is, the pursuit of equality necessarily will qualify someone's sense of what it means to be 'free'. Indeed, I suspect that the current concentration on these two 'values' keeps our society from pursuing the appropriate aims of a good society. Current understandings of 'freedom' and 'equality' tend to underwrite a view of society as essentially a collection of individuals who are engaged in continual bargaining procedures to provide mutual security without letting it cost too much in their personal freedom. Questions of the common purpose of such societies simply cannot be asked. Distinctions between society and state, while perfectly intelligible in a formal mode, make little empirical sense, because 'society' lacks a sufficient narrative to give it moral substance. The church, to be sure, has a stake in a 'limited state', but what keeps the state limited is not finally a theory about the place of the state within society but a people who have the power of discernment and know when to say 'No!'[16]

Thus, to say that the church must pursue societal justice is certainly right, but it is not very helpful or informative. For justice needs to be imaginatively construed and displayed by a people who have learned that genuine justice involves our receiving what is not due us! This justice is best served when such people exemplify in their own lives how to help one another—that is, how goods might be shared since no one has a rightful claim on them. A prerequisite for genuine justice is a sense of what might rightly be desired. Otherwise, justice remains formal and procedural. While there is much to be said for procedural norms, in themselves they can never sustain the conversation necessary for a people to survive as a good people.

Moreover, when freedom and equality are made ideal

abstractions, they become the justification for violence, since if these values are absent or insufficiently institutionalized some conclude that they must be forced into existence. As McDonagh points out, 'Most political orders are established by violence and certainly use violence to maintain themselves.' This is not without ethical justification, since, as McDonagh suggests, the state's hegemony of violence is at least in principle rooted in the just war rationale. The state uses violence to restrain those who have no respect for the lives and rights of other people in that society. Thus it seems the state can claim to use violence as the necessary means to preserve freedom and justice. And by further inference of this reasoning, when freedom and justice are missing, the Christian can resort to violence so that they may be achieved.

No one can deny the appeal of this position. Moreover, it certainly makes clear that the question of violence is the central issue for any Christian social ethic. Can Christians ever be justified in resorting to arms to do 'some good'? Are Christians not unjust if they allow another person to be injured or even killed if they might prevent that by the use of violence? Should not Christians call on the power of the state to employ its coercive force to secure more relative forms of justice? Such action would not be a question of using violence to be 'in control', but simply to prevent a worse evil.

Although I have sympathy with this position and though it certainly cannot be discounted as a possibility for Christians, one problem with many efforts to demonstrate the necessity of the use of violence is that they often misrepresent the character of the alternatives. Violence used in the name of justice, or freedom, or equality is seldom simply a matter of justice: it is a matter of the power of some over others. Moreover, when violence is justified in principle as a necessary strategy for securing justice, it stills the imaginative search for nonviolent ways of resistance to injustice.[18] For true justice never comes through violence, nor can it be based on violence. It can only be based on truth, which has no need to resort to violence to secure its own existence. Such a justice comes at best fitfully to nation-states, for by nature we are people who fear disorder and violence and thus we prefer order (even if the order is built on the lies inspired by our hates, fears, and resentments) to truth. The church, therefore, as a community based on God's kingdom of truth, cannot help but make all rulers tremble, especially when those rulers have become 'the people'.

Endnotes

1 The classic statement of this view remains G.H. Mead's *Mind, Self, and Society* (Chicago: University of Chicago Press, 1934).
2 John Howard Yoder, *The Original Revolution* (Scottdale, PA: Herald Press, 1971), 110; see the revised version of this essay in Yoder's *The Royal Priesthood: Essays Ecclesiological and Ecumenical* (Grand Rapids, MI:Eerdmans, 1994), 171. The reality designated 'world' is obviously an extremely complex phenomena. In the New Testament it is often used to designate that order organized and operating devoid of any reference to God's will. This is particularly true of the Johannine corpus. Yet the world is nonetheless described as the object of God's love (John 3:16) and even in 1 John, Jesus is called the 'saviour of the world' (4:14). Thus, even in the Johannine literature the world is not to assume that we have a clear idea of the empirical subject (i.e. government, society, etc.) that corresponds to the Johannine description. Yoder wisely locates the basis for the distinction between church and world in agents rather than ontological orders or institutions. To do so makes clear (1) that the distinction between church and world runs through every agent and thus there is no basis for self-righteousness on the part of those who explicitly identify with the church; and (2) that the 'necessities' many claim must be accepted as part and parcel of being 'world,' such as violence, are such only because of our faithfulness. Thus the world, when it is true to its nature as God's redeemed subject, can be ordered and governed without resort to violence.
3 I am obviously drawing here on the work of H.R. Niebuhr. See in particular *The Responsible Self* (New York: Harper and Row, 1963).
4 James Gustafson's *Treasures in Earthen Vessels* (New York: Harper and Row, 1961) still provides the best analysis of the church as a 'natural' institution. For the development of this insight, see Gustafson's too often overlooked *The Church as Moral Decision-Maker* (Philadelphia: Pilgrim Press, 1976). The general position I am trying to defend is nicely summarized by Karl Barth: 'The

decisive contribution which the Christian community can make to
the upbuilding and work and maintenance of the civil consists in
the witness which it has to give to it and to all human societies in
the form of the order of its own upbuilding and constitution. It cannot give in the world a direct portrayal of Jesus Christ, who is also
the world's Lord and Saviour, or of the peace and freedom and joy
of the kingdom of God. For it is itself only a human society moving
like all others to his manifestation. But in the form in which it exists
among them it can and must be to the world of men around it a
reminder of the law of the kingdom of God already set up on earth
in Jesus Christ, and a promise of its future manifestation. *De facto*,
whether they realize it or not, it can and should show them that
there is already on earth an order which is based on the great alter-
nation of the human situation and directed towards its manifestation' (Karl Barth, *Church Dogmatics*, IV/2, trans G.W. Bromiley
[Edinburgh, Scotland: T.&T. Clark, 1958], 72). A few pages later
Barth suggests that 'If the community were to imagine that the
reach of the sanctification of humanity accomplished in Jesus Christ
were restricted to itself and the ingathering of believers, that it did
not have corresponding effects *extra muros ecclesiae*, it would be in
flat contradiction to its own confession of its Lord' (723).

⁵ James Gustafson, *Christian Ethics and the Community* (Philadelphia:
Pilgrim Press, 1971), 153–63. That all human relations require and
engender some sense of trust indicates why the virtues require
narrative construal. For without the latter the very skills necessary
for us to be good can be made to serve our most destructive capacities. Sensing that, too often we try to avoid trusting anyone or
anything and, as a result, become subject to the most oppressive
tyrant: ourselves.

⁶ Thus, John Howard Yoder argues, 'Any renunciation of violence is
preferable to its acceptance; but what Jesus renounced is not first
of all violence, but rather the compulsiveness of purpose that
leads men to violate the dignity of others. The point is not that one
can attain all of one's legitimate ends without using violent
means. It is rather that our readiness to renounce our legitimate
ends whenever they cannot be attained by legitimate means itself
constitutes our participation in the triumphant suffering of the
Lamb.' *The Politics of Jesus* (Grand Rapids, MI: Eerdmans, 1972),
243–44.

⁷ Yoder, *The Original Revolution*, 121. It is instructive to compare this
with Michael Novak's critique of the Catholic bishops on nuclear
disarmament. Novak explicitly asserts that the 'Christian faith

does not teach us to rely on the miraculous' ('Making Deterrence Work,' *Catholicism in Crisis*, no. 1 [November 1982]: 5).

⁸ This way of putting the matter I have borrowed from Paul Van Buren's *Discerning the Way* (New York: Seabury Press, 1980).

⁹ As William Willimon says, 'The Lord's Supper is a "sanctifying ordinance", a sign of the continuity, necessity, and availability of God's enabling, communal, confirming, nurturing grace. Our characters are formed, sanctified, by such instruments of continual divine activity in our lives. Sanctification is a willingness to see our lives as significant only as we are formed into God's image for us. According to Paul, that image is always ecclesial, social, communal. In our attentiveness and response to this call to be saints, we find our thoughts, affections, sight, and deeds qualified by this beckoning grace. We become characterized as those who attend to the world in a different way from those who are not so qualified. Gradually we are weaned from our natural self-centered, autonomous ways of looking at the world until we become as we profess. We are different.' *The Service of God: How Worship and Ethics are Related* (Nashville, TN: Abingdon Press, 1983), 125.

¹⁰ Enda McDonagh, *Doing the Truth: The Quest for Moral Theology* (Notre Dame, IN: University of Notre Dame Press, 1979), 40–57.

¹¹ Vincent Donovan, *Christianity Rediscovered* (Maryknoll, NY: Orbis Books, 1982), 125. I am indebted to Philip Foubert for calling Donovan's fascinating book to my attention.

¹² Ibid., 127.

¹³ Enda McDonagh, *Church and Politics* (Notre Dame, IN: University of Notre Dame Press, 1980), 27.

¹⁴ Yoder, *The Original Revolution*, 165–66. For Yoder's fuller analysis of the theological status of democracy, see his 'The Christian Case for Democracy', *Journal of Religious Ethics* 5 (fall 1977): 209–24.

¹⁵ McDonagh, *Church and Politics*, 34.

¹⁶ McDonagh is quite right to stress the importance of the distinction between state and society, for there is no doubt it has proved crucial for securing more nearly just social orders. Moreover, there is every reason to think this distinction between state and society—that is, the assumption that society is a moral reality more primary than the organ of government, thus making the latter subordinate to, as well as in service to, the former—is the result of the Christian challenge to the authority of the Roman imperium. Yet it cannot therefore be concluded that the church has more stake in social orders that seem to maintain in theory a 'limited' state than in those that do not. For no state is more omnivorous in its

appetites for our loyalty that one that claims it is protecting our freedom from 'state control'. See ibid., 29–39.

[17] Ibid., 69.

[18] To what extent can Christians participate in a society's government? Any response will necessarily depend on the character of individual societies and their governments. Most governmental functions even within the military, do not depend on coercion and violence. It may be possible, therefore, for a Christian in some societies to be a policeman, prison warden, and so on. What is crucial, however, is that Christians work to help their societies develop the kind of people and institutions that make possible a government whose justice does not require resort to violence.

Chapter 7

How Common Worship Forms Local Character

Samuel Wells

This chapter attempts to show how the Eucharistic liturgy trains Christians in the moral imagination, in the habits, practices, notions and virtues of discipleship.[1] This is not what worship is for: worship isn't *for* anything—it is one of the few human activities conducted for its own sake. Our chief end, as the Westminster Confession reminds us, is 'to glorify God and enjoy him forever'.[2] Yet though worship has its own inner logic and intrinsic worth, it also prepares the disciple for witness and service. Each aspect of worship represents a vital dimension of moral formation. *Lex orandi, lex vivendi.*

What follows is a sequence of significant practices of Christian worship. The list is illustrative rather than exhaustive. Under each part of the liturgy I shall name skills that are taught, practices that are developed, habits that are formed, virtues that are acquired, and notions that are shaped. I shall then describe how this aspect of the liturgy has been performed in a local church and the character that has emerged from its repeated embodiment over time. The examples are not intended to be remarkable: on the contrary, their very ordinariness points to the way worship helps Christians take the right thing for granted.[3]

Gathering

When Christians gather together to worship, whether two or three, or two or three thousand, they are quickly reminded or become aware of three things. The first is that they are in the presence of God. The ability to name the presence of God is a skill. It is a skill that the Scriptures train the church to perform. The presence of God may be commanding, as for Abram in Haran; it may be troublesome or mysterious, as it was for Jacob at Bethel and Peniel; it can be echoingly silent, as for Elijah on Carmel, or awesome, as it was for Isaiah in the Temple. It can be perceived amid injustice, as for the centurion at the cross, or in human companionship, as for the disciples on the Emmaus Road.

By naming the presence of God the community develops the faculty of wonder. They have their imaginations stretched to perceive the greatness of God, the mystery of his deciding to make himself known, and the grace of his means of doing so. They are formed in the virtue of humility. They discover that this God has a purpose for his creation and that they themselves have a valued part to play—and they perceive that this story is not about them but about God. They learn to rest upon the notion of God's inextinguishable glory and unshakeable faithfulness. They enter a tradition of providence, encompassing Noah's rainbow, Isaac's ram, Moses' pillar of cloud, Hannah's prayer, Daniel's lions, Elizabeth's child, the stilled storm, the Great Commission, and the new Jerusalem. In the presence of God the congregation learn the skill of alertness, readiness, anticipation, expectation: that the God who has acted, and keeps his promises, will reveal himself today.

At much the same time as the congregation become aware of the presence of God, they become aware of the presence of one another. They discover that the body of Christ has many members, and they learn about the diversity of the gifts that the Holy Spirit has given the body. They are reminded that those gifts are for the building up of the church and that the neglect of any of the gifts is to the detriment of the body. They realize the discipline of forming an identity separate from the world, a light, before once again retuning to serve the world, as salt. By committing themselves to meet regularly together Christians practice the skills of politics, the nonviolent resolution of conflicting goods in corporate life. They practice the habits of welcoming the stranger, and valuing the child. By faithfully meeting week by week the congregation are formed in the virtue of constancy. By making Sunday the focal day the congregation learn the skill of telling the time, of distinguishing the important from the urgent, of realizing that God has given us enough time to do what he calls us to do. By taking time to worship they are formed in the virtue of patience.

More gradually, the congregation become aware of those who are not gathering together—those who are absent. Some are worshipping elsewhere; some have died; some are sick or unable to present; some are estranged or hiding from God and/or the Church; some have never been invited; some have never heard; some have hardened or bruised or bewildered hearts. This is how the community develops the skill of memory for those who are no longer here, and awareness of the breadth of the body and the extent of the kingdom. This awareness shapes the practices of pastoral care and evangelism. It fosters the virtue of love for the lost. It gives substance to the notion of the communion of saints, whose constant worship of God the congregation join from time to time.

One local congregation chose to embody this last notion, the communion of saints, through a photography project. They sought to surround the area used for worship with photographs of notable characters, all of whom lived in the area around the church, but none of whom came to worship on a Sunday. A group of single mothers, who used the church for a weekly art class, identified the people concered, shot, developed, and mounted the photographs, and displayed them around the church. Thus the worshipping congregation were surrounded on the Sunday with those for whom they prayed. When a bid went from the neighborhood to the government for large sums of urban regeneration funding, there was a sudden search for photographs that expressed what was good about the community. The photographs on the church walls were ideal for the purpose, and were duly used. Thus had the local church's faithful notion of gathering to worship helped a neighborhood realize its human worth.

Confessing

When Christian come kneeling and humble before God in confession, they learn what it means to come naked and humbled before God in baptism. They thus prepare themselves to come naked and humble before God in death. They develop the skill of naming their own sin. They learn the savage blinding power of self-deception. They see themselves in the brother's speechlessness before Joseph, David's incomprehension before Nathan, and Peter's horror as the cock crowed. By confessing their sin corporately they recognize their participation in wider ignorance, selfishness, and pride, in human and global fear and finitude. In resolving to sin no more the congregation register the weight of making promises that they may not be able to keep, and practice the habit of dependence on the grace of God. By bringing their confession to an end and handing their sin over in penitence, they are formed in the virtue of humility, for they must realize that the worst that they have done cannot alter God's love for them or his working out of his eternal purpose, and that they cannot wrest their destiny, or that of those they have hurt, out of his hands. The congregation practice the virtue of courage, in anticipating their own death, and faith, in committing themselves to the one who judges justly. In receiving absolution they inhabit the clothes of their baptism. They learn the notions of adoption by the Father, justification through the Son, new birth in the Spirit, liberation from slavery, the resurrection of the body, and vocation to a life of prayer and service. They realize that salvation is a gift to be received, not a reward to be earned.

In one local congregation there was an elderly woman who had lived all her life in the neighborhood. She had attended the church longer than anyone could remember—perhaps fifty years. Everyone in the church, from the wildest child to the oldest salt, loved and revered her. One day, during worship, she was asked why she attended church so faithfully. She was a person of action rather than words, and her life had been devoted to care rather than cleverness. Without pause, she simply responded, 'For my sins'. There was silence. If she, who was holy, came for her sins, where did that place everyone else? Clearly her joy came from knowing God's forgiveness, and her faithfulness came from knowing that that grace could be found nowhere else. When she died, the congregation realized that she had symbolized everything they believed in. In her gentle way she expressed that she had been formed by the worship in which she had shared.

Listening

When Christians listen for God's word in Scripture, they learn to listen for God's word in every conversation. They develop the skill of storytelling, of finding their place and role in the story. They grow in the ability to recognize beginnings and endings, to perceive how God sows his seed and reaps his harvest. They learn to see the author at work, noting the house style of exalted meek and dejected mighty. The congregation learn also the skill of listening, of taking in the whole of God, action, interpretation, intention. They realize how much there is to discover, and they practice fitting their own small story into the larger story of God. They are formed in the virtue of prophetic hope, the conviction that God has acted before to save his people and the trust that he will act again to set them free. They learn the notion of revelation, the belief that truth and meaning are communicated from God's side of the conversation. They grow in an understanding of truth, that accounts can be accurate, trustworthy and worthy of commitment. They practice communal discernment, as together they use their gifts to hear the word speak in their contemporary context. They learn the discipline of authority and obedience. They come to see history as theology teaching by examples. And they realize what it means to inhabit a tradition.

In one local congregation a custom has developed at the evening service. After the second reading the priest asks a question of the congregation that links with the Scripture passage. The question does not seek a right or wrong answer

but invites members to share their experience. It might be, 'I
wonder if you have know someone with a disability'; or, 'I
wonder who you think really runs the country.' The sermon
that follows usually weaves some of these answers into a pres-
entation of the Word and in insight into the character of God
and the practice of the church. Sometimes members of the congregation add observations at the end. On one occasion the
priest was particularly pleased with what he had in mind to
say and forgot to ask the wondering question. The following
morning an outraged member of the congregation sought him
out. 'Last night', she said, 'you simply talked at us for fully
fifteen minutes, and then just stopped. There was no opportunity for discussion whatsoever.' The priest, somewhat defen-
sively and ironically, pointed out that this would have been
her experience of worship every Sunday if she attended almost
any other church both in that city and quite possibly throughout the world. Yet here was a woman, living in a deprived
community, who had through the repeated practice of listening and discerning, come to take for granted that her experience was an important part of the proclamation of God's word,
that she had a place in God's story. This was an assumption—
a form of her faith—that liturgical habit had taught her. It
helped her to see the unique opportunity her church was offering to its community—to find their story in God's story.

Interceding

When a congregation intercede together, they put themselves in
place of others before God. They develop the skill of distinguishing pain from sin, as they come to separate what needs
intercession from what needs confession. They learn the skill of
distinguishing suffering from evil, as they perceive the difference between a call for God's mercy and a call for God's justice.
They learn to distinguish need from want, as, like Israel before
them, they discern what it is to be God's beloved, and how that
differs from being like other nations. They practice the virtue of
patience, as they come to understand that all bad things come to
an end in God's time, and that God has prepared for those who

love him such things as pass their understanding. They learn the virtue of persistence, as they look back over years of knocking on heaven's door, and see that change did come in South Africa, peace, of a kind, did come in Ireland, and so it must in God's mercy somehow come in Palestine. They are also shaped in the virtue of prudence, for they learn only to request what they can cope with receiving. Prudence helps the congregation see the difference between what God can do and what they believe it is in the character of God to do. They learn the notion of providence as they look back and see how God's hand has guided his flock from age to age. They deepen their understanding of the kingdom of God, as they look for God's ways with the world that go way beyond the breadth of the church. They learn what it means to have an advocate before the Father.

In one local congregation a woman who often attended the Sunday evening service began attending an adult literacy class held in the church on a weekday. It became clear that she had never learned to read well. To help her grow in confidence, she was asked to read a lesson every third Sunday. She was encouraged simply to miss out the longer or unfamiliar words or names, and concentrate on the ones she could read confidently. Gradually her range of words increased. Eventually she was asked to lead prayers. She felt she could not do this spontaneously, as some other did, so she would spend the week asking people to jot down prayers for her to use, which she would then carefully type into word processor, which she was learning to use on another adult education class. For her, leading intercessions was the summit of her years of attending church. She realized that this was the moment when she was like Jesus, standing before the Father bringing the people with her. It was also like the anticipated moment of her death, when she would stand face to face with God, and he would ask her, 'Where are all the others?'—and she could reply, 'Here, in my prayers'.

Sharing peace

By having to share the peace before sharing the bread, Christians learn that reconciliation is a necessary to their lives as their daily bread. They develop the skill of admonition. When the desire to love is at least as great as the desire to tell the truth, admonition is an important practice. It affirms that Christians have nothing to fear from the truth, and that protecting others from the truth is seldom a statement of faith. Sharing the peace also develops in the congregation the habit of not letting the sun go down on their anger, of seeing the naming of resentment as the first step in the forming of a new relationship based on healing and forgiveness rather than tolerance and turning a blind eye. They practice the virtues of mercy and forbearance, virtues that depend on the knowledge that they too have sinned and been forgiven, that they too have grown through constructive criticism, that they too have moods and quirks and prejudices. They grow in the virtues of humility and honesty, virtues that rest on the realization that the Christian life is not about arriving at perfection, but about making interesting mistakes on the way. They are formed in the virtues of patience and courage, which help them to try once more with challenging relationships and risk rejection by trying to reconcile. They learn the notion of forgiveness, the astonishing story of how the prodigal was not just received home but treated like a king. They learn again what it means for the baptized to be a body and for its members all to function. They learn the ultimate unity of grace and truth.

In one local congregation the intimate connection between reconciliation with God and with one another is brought out by the use of a human statue. Two members of the congregation are invited to kneel opposite one another in the centre of the church and rest their respective heads on one another's left shoulder. (Those who participate, often one adult and one child, must be self-nominated – efforts to nominate one's neighbor are rejected.) The statue affirms that one cannot be reconciled with God until one is reconciled with one's neighbor.

The statue also affirms the physical nature of the healing of that body. One local congregation had a parish away day during which a litany of complaints, anxious frustrations, and a sense of helplessness about one aspect of the church's ministry rained down upon those responsible. That day, when the time came for the Holy Communion, the peace was shared without words – the simple handshake and holding of eye contact was a statement of trust and commitment and reconciliation after perhaps too many words had been said. In being able to share the peace after such a traumatic day, the congregation discovered that it was possible to name the truth without fear.

Sharing communion

By sharing bread with one another around the Lord's table, Christians learn to live in peace with those with whom they share other tables—breakfast, shopfloor, office, checkout. They develop the skills of distribution, of the poor sharing their bread with the rich, and the rich with the poor. They develop the skills of inclusion, of perceiving that diversity only enriches integrity. Everyone is called to a place around the table, whatever their gender, their race, their class, whatever their orientation, their physical health or ability, their mental health or ability, whatever their social or criminal history. They develop the practices of offering and receiving. They hand over the first fruits of labour and receive back the first fruits of the resurrection. They learn what is meant by a gift, by offering their food and drink and money to God and allowing him to do whatever he wants with them. They develop the skills of participating in the life of heaven, in realizing their simple actions anticipate God's eternal destiny. They learn to look around them as they eat, and speculate on whether these are the people with whom God predicts they will spend eternity, or whether he has other people in mind, and if so, why those people are not present now. The congregation practice the virtue of justice, as they ensure that all are treated with equal respect, and all have their role and place around the throne of God. They learn the virtue of generosity, as they realize that they have freely received more than enough from God, and can therefore freely give. They are shaped in the virtue of hope, as they are given a picture of what the heavenly banquet will be like. They learn the notion of regular dependence on God's abiding providence, as they realize they live not on bread alone, but on every word that comes from the mouth of God. They perceive that at the heart of fellowship is sacrifice. They discover that holiness is formation as a kingdom of priests, a community through whom God makes his name know in the world, a people who are what they eat—the body of Christ.

One local congregation found it difficult to decide whether they should sit, stand, or kneel to receive communion. Kneeling seemed appropriate to some, because it embodied humility. But some said that, without an altar rail, it asked too much of people with disabilities. It seemed that sitting was the posture that stressed equality, because everybody looked and felt much the same. But it was felt that, besides being too comfortable, remaining in one's seat suggested that God made the whole journey, with almost no response from his people. Standing in circle became the norm. It stresses the difference of height, age and physical ability, and it made it necessary for some to rest on the strength of others. Though some said they felt unworthy to stand, others pointed out that the Christ had enabled, even commanded them to stand, and that standing was a symbol of resurrection. By standing in a circle, the congregation realized they did not just eat of one body—they *were* one body.

Being sent out

Finally when Christians are sent back out into the world they learn what it means to be salt and light, to be distinct yet among. They develop the practice of service, remembering that even the Son of Man came not to be served but to serve. They learn the habit of partnership, remembering that those who are not against Christ are with him. They practice seeking out ways of God in the most benighted corners of the world. They learn the disciplines and techniques of co-operating with people of very different principles and stories, of resolving conflict without violence, and standing beside the weak and afflicted. They work out the virtue of justice, in seeking the equality they experienced at the Lord's table. They develop the habit of peacemaking, seeking the reconciliation they experienced before they came to the Lord's table. They practice the virtue of temperance, learning to expect compromise and to be changed by those they seek to influence. They experience the cost of the virtue of love. They inhabit the notion of mission, as like the seventy they go out in order to bring back stories of what the Spirit has done. They learn the practice of witness, as they realize how the Church differs from the world and how to speak despite this difference. They explore the meaning of incarnation, as they translate their experience of the body of Christ into their context of home, work, and leisure. And they discover again the notion of kingdom, that for all their mistakes, God will work his purpose out in ways beyond their imaginations.

In one local church the notices used to come just before the sending out. On one occasion the priest shared with the congregation that a group of young girls had been trying for several days to persuade him to allow them to use the church building to dance in on a Saturday. He asked the congregation for suggestions. After a pause, one woman aged eighty-six put up her hand and said, 'I'll sit with them if you like.' After a few weeks, one of the girls' mothers took over and set up a dance club that flourished for three years. Challenged by the call to go and do likewise, the elderly woman proved to be a stirring example to the rest of the congregation. If an eighty-six-year-old could be a youth worker, everyone could.

Concluding words

Worshipping together does not always feel like moral formation. It is about the ordinary and mundane, about habit and repetition, and learning over time to take the right things for granted. In many churches, people feel that the practice of worship has departed considerably from any conscious embodiment of the virtues described here. But in almost all cases, when habit and memory are still alive, the potential for renewal is still high. And a strange thing happens when, at a public, secular gathering, people begin to articulate the need for their institution to divert from its daily business, name divisions and mistakes, tell stories and affirm mission statements, name needs, be reconciled, and share food in order to be re-empowered for service of the community. Members of the church may choose whether or not to claim a copyright, but at the very least they will raise an eyebrow. They may well wonder at this rediscovery of the church's heritage, and be consoled that imitation is the sincerest form of flattery.[4]

Endnotes

[1]   I owe this way of understanding the ethical dimensions of the liturgy to Stanley Hauerwas. See his 'The Liturgical Shape of the Christian Life: Teaching Christian Ethics as Worship', In *Good Company: The Church as Polis* (Notre Dame, Ind.: University of Notre Dame Press, 1995), 153-68.

[2]   'The Westminster Shorter Catechism', in *The Presbyterian Church (USA) Book of Confessions* (Louisville, KY: Office of the General Assembly, 1983), Q.1.

[3]   The ordinariness of the examples of Stanley Hauerwas's ecclesiology. Both David Fergusson and Robin Gill suggest Hauerwas's church is in large measure a fantasy, or is inevitably of implicitly a rare Mennonite phenomenon. It is my experience and contention that this is not the case. See David Ferguson, *Community, Liberalism and Christian Ethics* (Cambridge: Cambridge University Press, 1999); and Robin Gill, *Churchgoing and Christian Ethics* (Cambridge: Cambridge University Press, 2001).

[4]   I am grateful to John Sweet and the Readers Summer Course 2001, to Stephen Barton and the Society for the Study of Christian Ethics Conference 2001, and in particular to Jolyon Mitchell, Luke Bretherton, and John Inge for their reflections on earlier versions of this essay. A number of people have suggested that 'Doxology' in the form of music and hymns should form part of this pattern. This essay sets out to address the sequential aspects of the liturgy and I confess I have not yet found a way to integrate the pervasive aspects of worship without losing the simplicity of the essay's shape. I would welcome suggestions on this.

Chapter 8

Roundtable on Evangelicalism and Virtue Ethics 2[1]

Luke Bretherton, Steve Chalke, Shane Claiborne,
Stanley Hauerwas, Russell Rook, Samuel Wells

Luke Bretherton:
I think life and death would be a good place to start this conversation. In your work, Stanley, you've highlighted the point that Christians don't know how to die, that we haven't really thought about how death relates directly to the central parts of our faith. If Jesus is Lord and Christ is King, and all of time and life is fulfilled in Christ, we should live in the light of that reality rather than in the attempt to control our lives. The attempt to have ever tighter regimes of managing and controlling our bodies and our lives and all the rest of it, is rendered irrelevant at death. One of the really profound things that comes out of your work is how things like modern medicine develop hugely sophisticated techniques and regimes of control over the human body because it exists in a culture which thinks death is the worst thing possible.

Health is an interesting case for other reasons too. You see that the problems we were discussing in our first conversation are not just Christian or evangelical problems. Our culture relies on stakes in the ground rather than virtues. In medicine, you have codes of ethics. Instead of training nurses to be virtuous nurses and taking the time to apprentice them in the practices of excellent nursing, there are codes and procedures about what to do.

In a sense, evangelicalism is just displaying a central crisis in our culture. Whether it's medicine, education, or whatever else, everyone's suffering from the same thing. There's a shift from profession as *confession* to profession as *technique* and procedure. A confession requires faith in a vision; this is the old medieval understanding which guided law, medicine, education, etc. You needed certain virtues and disciplines in order to fulfil the vision of what good health, education, etc. consisted of. A vocation was a confession of faith in a particular vision. Today, the system defines a profession as a set of competencies and techniques policed by a set of legal procedures and codified standards. Virtuous, Christian modes of caring in service professions witness to a different, but profoundly relevant mode of caring. But we shouldn't stop at this question; we want to get onto the question of how we are sick or how we suffer. It's something that is a crucial thing to explore.

Russell Rook:
I think there are essentially two issues here. Firstly, there's the issue that people don't know how to die well. So we want to take control of death in order to reduce our fear. We either feel we've got a right to be kept going as long as humanly possible or we want to determine the exact time or conditions of our passing through assisted suicide or euthanasia. That presents another bunch of ethical challenges for Christians.

But secondly, there's this issue: The National Health Service (NHS) in the UK was designed to be a system of uni-

versal healthcare which society owned universally; the idea being that everyone contributed and everyone benefited. Over time this view has shifted. While the method of funding has remained largely the same—the NHS is paid for by UK taxpayers—the attitude that citizens have toward it has altered. For most, the provision of universal healthcare is the *government's* responsibility. Regardless of the complications and costs involved in supplying ever more sophisticated treatments and therapies, the citizens of the UK consider it the government's responsibility to keep them in the very best health. Public health is no longer thought to be our own collective responsibility as a society.

My question is this: how do Christians in such a context recover a sense of responsibility for one another's health as opposed to an expectation that 'the state will sort us out' if we get into a bind? If part of our role as the church is to demonstrate God's plan to heal a fallen world, this would seem particularly important. I'm interested to know a bit more about what you do, Shane, in a community where you don't have a universal health service to fall back on.

Shane Claiborne:
Well, we had sort of a youthful innocence when we moved into the neighbourhood in Philadelphia. We didn't really think about health insurance and then our mothers started asking us: 'What are you going to do if you get sick?' After a certain point, our health care answer couldn't be 'Call my parents.'

I'll never forget one of my first experiences in my neighbourhood. One of the five year-old kids that I'd grown really, really close to had chronic asthma, like a lot of the kids in the neighbourhood. Every time she had an asthma attack she had to go to the emergency room and wait for hours and hours to be seen. During one of those emergency room runs, she died. Five years old, she died of an asthma attack. In America, if you don't have a family doctor, you can't get treatment.

Stanley Hauerwas:
That's because emergency wards are where the poor in America get served and they have to wait.

Shane Claiborne:
There are so many things that happen as a result of this system of dealing with the poor. People can't pay their bills and hospitals go bankrupt. Two of the three hospitals in my

neighbourhood have gone bankrupt in the last ten years. Now the lines for treatment are even longer.

This situation raises all kinds of questions, in my mind; a lot of them are ecclesiological questions. I'm excited that conversations are happening on a national level, but I also believe that we just can't tell the government to do what the church is commissioned to do. So, actually even before I was around, a group of folks in the Midwest didn't want to wait for

Washington, D.C. to solve the health care problem. They started pooling their money and saying: 'We're going to meet each other's medical bills.' It sounds a lot like Acts 2 and 4; the vision spread and before long it had grown from just a few hundred people to thousands. Now, I've joined that cooperative. In fact I'm kind of in the core.

Russell Rook:
So do you pay in a sum of money every month like a health plan?

Shane Claiborne:
Every month we get a newsletter of who's in the hospital. We pray for each other and then we pull our money together to get bills paid. We've done over $500,000,000—half a billion dollars—since 1993. Every year we pull together about $12,000,000 dollars and over 90% of it goes directly to medical bills. It's not just a financial initiative; there's also a relational aspect that I really like. Ultimately, it's a pretty good option and for a lot of us, it's how we do healthcare.

Luke Bretherton:
Basically, we are faced with two healthcare options: either you leave it all up to the market or you look to the government to solve the problem. But actually, there's this whole tradition

which seems to be central to Methodism and things like the early labour movement in which the church was very involved. The question of this movement was: 'What does it mean for us to have mutually responsible, faithful, committed relationships in which family is the paradigm?' The answer to this question works itself out in things like the origin of social insurance, the co-operative movement, and mutual-based banking.

One of the issues that evangelicals often bump up against is a false division between evangelism and social action. A vision of full reconciliation—God drawing all creation into His embrace—is as much about healing and repair of the world as it is about telling people the good news. You have to articulate and locate what you're doing within a bigger story. As you say Shane, it began with ecclesiology; it began with asking: 'What does it mean to be the church?' Being church doesn't mean just doing what we do on Sunday, but re-imagining a whole range of activities from how we provide mortgages or housing for people, to social insurance, healthcare and so on. That is why Christians set up hospitals, hospices and the like.

Shane Claiborne:
The way that many people in our community do healthcare is clearly a response to the system in the US, but this kind of thing happens all around the world. There's another cooperative that we started called 'The Relational Tithe'. We're a group of Christians globally that have committed to give 10% of our incomes into a common fund that distributes things according to people's needs. I mean a lot of the idea for it came from a theologian from the UK—Ray Mayhew—who wrote a paper called 'Embezzlement: The Sin of the Contemporary Church.' He looks at how offerings have been really spread to staff and buildings.

His article sparked this idea to put our money together and respond to people's needs in the neighbourhood. We found that now there are clusters all over the globe that model this same concept.

When there was a need that came up in our neighbourhood and we put our money together at The Simple Way, we didn't come up with much. But The Relational Tithe steps in when there are non-medical needs in our community. We help throw birthday parties for folks that have never had one, send people on vacation, replace water heaters, get people out of junk law suits, help Miss Betty when her house catches on fire. All these needs are met and it's become a part of our witness.

When our corner store was robbed at gunpoint, we were able to take an offering from the neighbourhood, but it wasn't much so we supplemented it with a gift from The Relational Tithe. The money collected plus the gift replaced all of the money that was stolen from the shop. When we presented the money, we said: 'This is a gift from the church. We're a bunch of brothers and sisters that believe in bearing each other's burdens. You had something really unfair happen to you and we want to carry that with you.'

Steve Chalke:
On the UK side, we run into some different problems trying to work with local communities often because of tensions with government. We get a lot of money from government for some of the schemes we run; let's take the example of education. We receive funding from central government for education who tell us that our task is to turn around the failure of past decades through innovation. However, the problem is that government has already narrowly defined what they believe education is and how they will measure success. Therefore there is huge pressure to use your money to produce the outcomes that they expect.

We see the world differently. Take two small examples. We know that getting into the habit of cleaning your teeth after lunch is going to mean that they won't rot in your head, that you will have a better lifestyle, and that you will also learn wider lessons about managing yourself and your health along the way, not to mention saving a huge health bill in future years etc. So we put time and money into developing a teeth cleaning program as part of our curriculum and we got canned by government for doing it—for being too 'soft' around our educational outcomes.

Or, we know that a child will thrive in school if we also work with their mum or dad, or both, if we get the opportunity. If we can boost their sense of self-esteem and self-worth; increase their understanding of the role they play in their child's educational development, their child will fare better in life and stand a greater chance of getting off the poverty conveyer belt. But, this takes money and time. It is a big investment. The problem is that government wants instant results. So, we are in a battle—a constant battle with government around the definitions of education and health.

As the church, we can only define what justice or peace is through an understanding of who God is. It's equally true, for health or education; we can only understand what these things are because of our understanding of God. Therefore, we will be in conflict, or tension, with government as much as working with them. Perhaps this is the most healthy form of partnership.

Talking about social service provision, Sam, you had mentioned something about the way in which the church often justifies itself and gains plausibility through social service provision. A part of me thinks: 'OK, so what? What's the problem with that view?' All of this stuff is a witness. Having said that, I recognise that some evangelicals probably think: 'That's just the social gospel, it has nothing to do with being witnesses. Isn't all of this just a way of getting around telling people about Jesus?' How would you respond to that?

Sam Wells:
In the end, Jesus wept over Jerusalem. The real question is whether we love these people. Because if we love these people, we take very, very seriously what's to become of them. It's about people's well-being. Salvation and well-being are pretty much wrapped up in each other.

Theologically, I think there are three categories of evangelism: priestly evangelism, kingly evangelism, and prophetic evangelism. *Prophetic* evangelism points to God and points to the world saying: 'The world is not the church.' *Priestly* evangelism tries to embody in its own life what only God's love can do. It's being a living example, but also involves making humble partnerships with other people who are going some of that journey with you. For example, the kinds of activities involved in a hospital are churchly activities. They are assisting practices, 'Good Samaritan' practices, discipleship practices. Sure they've become formulaic and professionalised and all of those things, but sometimes we find that journeying together is really as important as anything else. As you all know, it isn't the outcome, it's sticking with the process of regeneration and trying to redefine and refine that process every few weeks. That's where a bit of humility comes in, we don't always know what the end should be.

At a conference that I went to, they asked a question: 'If you saw a starving man in the desert, would you give him a loaf of bread or Bible?' This pre-supposes that we are wandering through deserts, that we are seeing people who are literate and who are capable of reading a Bible, and that they are not so starving that they can't process the bread, whether that be the Bible or the food. It's nonsense to think that we have to choose between those two options. The point of really caring for people is that you care for the *whole* of life. Priestly evangelism is having humility about our knowledge and ability; it's being incarnate, not being ashamed of our own humanity. The activities of priestly evangelism, being with the sick, are good things in themselves. They are the stained glass windows of the gospel. They are the life that is made possible by knowing one is being saved. You've got to offer something. Why would anyone be a Christian unless the church is giving them living examples of what new life through Christ leads to.

Steve Chalke:
What about the third kind of evangelism?

Sam Wells:
Well, the third type is *kingly* evangelism, which is basically making people behave Christianly when they've already said

they don't really want to be Christians. I don't think we should institutionalise those Christian commitments. I think kingly evangelism is almost always a disaster.

Stanley Hauerwas:
I'd like to change the subject just a little to a pastoral practice that I think is crucial that will help people know how to talk about dying. I think ministers are not well schooled to help people recognise that they are going to die. We need to learn to pray and train people to do funerals well. We need to embrace the liturgical shaping that includes the community in celebration of a life. It's really very important for all of us. It will help us to learn how to make that journey to death. So often funerals seem to say: 'They're not really dead.'

Sam Wells:
The word 'celebration' is a key word in terms of what's going on at funerals. On my father's side, my aunts, my grandmother, and so on, are more on the evangelical end of the church. My aunt's funeral was in an evangelical church. I actually had a very uncomfortable experience, partly for a good reason. I'll try to explain.

In the last twenty years or so we've seen a clear movement from an 'impersonal funeral', which is about the future, to a 'personal funeral', which is a celebration of the past, and the denial that the person has actually died. In American funerals you almost never see the coffin; at Duke Chapel, it's usually a memorial service. We don't want to see the coffin but we do want to see a big photograph of the guy. Yes, it's personal, but unless the preacher does the work of saying: 'These are the ways in which this person's life showed us the face of God. It doesn't matter about their mistakes, we learn as much by their mistakes as by their successes.'— Unless the preacher does that

work, the funeral denies the resurrection or at least cheapens it.

I found my aunt's funeral particularly uncomfortable because the pastor who took the service just talked about the resurrection and seemed incapable of recognising that she died in a very painful, uncomfortable way. There was no sadness in the funeral. Sadness is clearly part of the gospel, but his general emphasis in the funeral was right. 1 Corinthians 15 is a very good passage to read. People don't like it because it doesn't seem personal.

I think how we do funerals is extremely significant. One of the most moving funerals that I've attended was for my autistic cousin. It was perfect because it was about resurrection, but it was in a place where my cousin had been loved and accepted for who he was. This is Jesus. This is transforming the pain of autism in this person's life into something very beautiful.

Luke Bretherton:
This all goes back to the story that we're living, it goes back to the issue of what we are aspiring to live for. We live in a culture that does everything to avoid pain. We think that pain cannot teach us anything about how to live a good life, whether it's the pain of withdrawing from the TV or the pain of cancer. We really believe that pain has no way of helping us to be human. Why have we lost the art of bearing pain? Why is so much of medicine's work about keeping people from ever experiencing any kind of pain?

Stanley Hauerwas:
The question that we need to consider is how to begin to recognize that we're embodied; that the body is a gift, but that it also destines us to death. How can we recognise bodily life as it should be? How do we live with one another's pains as gifts?

Some churches have prayers where people pray for one another. You rarely hear: 'I've got cancer, so please help me.' We need to think about what it means to expose the body and its vulnerability. Part of the building up of the body of Christ includes thinking about what kinds of care we receive as we make our way to death.

Luke Bretherton:
A good starting illustration is: You're sitting, working late at night, and you've got a headache and some back pain. Instead of asking yourself: 'Why am I in pain?', you take a headache pill with coffee because that allows you to do another two hours worth of work. We short circuit the pain to stop ourselves from asking: 'Why am I sitting here working late at night? What environment or context makes me happier working here at night rather than going to bed earlier with my spouse? Is my boss terrorizing me? Why have I become so anxious about my work environment that I feel I need to work so late?'

There's a whole bunch of questions we might ask, but the ability to reach for the coffee and headache pill short circuits that process. Pain doesn't interrupt the flow that is dominated by a whole range of underlying emotional or work wrangles, or political and economic conditions but which we never engage with. This is all taking place as people sit doing their emails.

There can be a romanticization of pain, a belief that pain is inherently redemptive. I don't think it's redemptive in a strong sense—it won't save you, but it does render you more vulnerable and teaches you about what it means to be human. We start utterly vulnerable and dependent as babies and wind up vulnerable and dependent as old people. There's this tiny little window when you can operate as an autonomous being and there's this illusion that that window is the normal bit. Pain interrupts our autonomy; it tells us that autonomy isn't normal. We seem to have all sorts of mechanisms that stop us from learning that basic truth about what it means to be human.

Shane Claiborne:
There is redemptive suffering and then there's stupid, senseless suffering. Living without a fear of death is something that we've been learning in my community. One of my community mates, a social worker, was in one of her clients' home cleaning. The client had really bad Alzheimer's and was not able to live on her own. As she was cleaning the house, she found a prayer written by the woman named Gwen that said: 'Dear God, help me never die in a nursing home.'

So my community mate, the social worker, came back to talk to her husband about the situation and they decided to basically adopt Gwen, without knowing how long she would survive. Gwen lived about seven years. She died last month, but as they lived together, they learned so much; it was a constant adventure. Gwen's brain got into a cycle; every 10 seconds and she would ask: 'Where are we?' And they would say: 'Well, we're in Switzerland now.' Ten seconds later: 'Where are we? Where are we?' and the answer: 'In Brazil'.

It was such a quirky family. They all lived in a rough part of town together, the social worker, the husband Darren, the son Justus and the adopted old granny, Gwen. Their family just radiated hospitality and love. As Gwen got sicker and sicker, they had to make a decision: 'Are we going to try to do everything we can to put things in her body and keep her breathing longer?'

Instead, we had a powerful moment of remembering the past and the future and celebrating her life. We had an incredible time together, telling stories about her and singing with her and holding her hand. Justus, the little four year old, was there, and it was an illustration of what we've been learning about helping people die well.

In communities like the Bruderhof or the Hutterites, I've seen people die and the community will spend the whole night holding a vigil candle light service and singing at the person's window. It's never even an issue of what technology they need to keep living.

One of the times we were in India, I worked every afternoon in the Home for the Dying, Mother Theresa's first home. Every day we would go into the streets and we would bring people that were dying into the house and they would die. The amazing thing was, it was one of the few places where it felt like death had really lost its sting. In the Home for the Dying, people were singing, people were laughing together. One of the nurses had complained that some of the patients would not have died if they could have just had an IV. Mother Theresa would say: 'Our goal is not to keep them alive but to help them to die well, with dignity and with love.'

Maybe they could have used another IV, but I think that the point was that, in that place, we don't fear death. We're not just trying to keep people breathing, but help them to live the last few moments of their life with love and community. When you go into the morgue in the Home for the Dying in Calcutta, it says on the wall: 'I'm on my way to heaven', but when you walk out of the morgue, above the door it says: 'Thanks for helping me get here.' I think that's really what the resurrection is about, laughing at death's power.

Russell Rook:
That's it! In these stories we glimpse the inner logic of the gospel. A logic that directly contradicts so much of the culture that we live in, the culture that says pain and death are at best meaningless. Mother Theresa understood what all Christians need to know, namely, that death isn't meaningless at all. After all, it is one man's death that saves the world. For this reason, facing the reality of death is something that Christians share with Christ himself.

Two years ago now, Nicola, the pastor of my local church died. Since then, I've often reflected on her death. She had suffered from cancer for 18 months. Obviously, as an evangelical charismatic church, we prayed for healing many, many times, but somewhere along the way, we got to a point at the end when we began to prepare for her death rather than simply expect a miraculous healing to happen. Having lived very well, Nicola died very well, and, in this, she taught us more as a church than we ever could have learned through a miraculous healing. I had the privilege of joining the family for a few hours on that last afternoon. Around her bedside, family and friends sat singing songs, telling stories, praying, laughing, crying. None of this is to underestimate the pain of Nicola's death for the many people who loved and mourned her, but in that hospital room, I discovered what Shane discovered in Calcutta, namely, that in Christ, death has lost its sting.

That year, I had written a book on the hope of resurrection entitled, *A Certain Rumour: Learning to Live Hopefully Ever After*, I dedicated the book to Nicola. In those last months and days she taught me what every minister should teach their congregation.

There was something about Nicola's death that taught us to learn to live hopefully, and it was only her death that could have done it. A miraculous healing would not have taught us to live hopefully ever after. It would have only increased the modern illusion that we can cheat death, whether by the modern marvels of medical science or a prayer for healing. Once again, I don't offer this theological observation glibly as I know that, in her absence, Nicola's family and friends continue to pay an enormous price for the lesson that she has taught.

The truth is that the gospel story, the best news ever told, doesn't shy away from death. In fact, far from it, the story embraces death in order to deal with it once and for all. As it gives way to resurrection, death itself finds new meaning. It is essential that we teach people to die well because this is something that they share with Christ. As Paul himself points out, if we want to know Christ, we must be ready to become like him in his death (Phil 3:10).

Stanley Hauerwas:

Rich Mouw, the president of Fuller Theological Seminary tells this story: At the time he was teaching at Calvin College and there was a Calvinist community in Grand Rapids, Michigan. They were pretty young and they lived in the poor part of the city. One of the community members was a doctor and the other was a young architect. The young architect and his wife had just had their first child, but he found out that he had severe cancer of the spine.

Rich was in the room with the young architect. When the doctor came in, the young architect said: 'Well, they've done all the testing and the radiologist people tell me they can do

this and the chemotherapy people tell me they can do this. What do you think I ought to do?' The doctor, who was part of the community, said: 'Well, they can do those therapies, but quite frankly you're very sick. You might get another six months if you do one or the other of them, but you're not going to live beyond that. Basically, they're going to experiment to try to learn something for future patients. I want you to know that if you're ready to die, we're ready to be with you as you die. Don't worry, your wife and your child will not be abandoned.' The young man decided not to do anything and he died within a month. Just think how rare that is, for people to be able to speak to one another that way.

Steve Chalke:
What do we do with people who will critique us and say that we have no faith because we should be praying for that man's healing? The kind of people who argue that what the specialist says he can do is irrelevant; really we should be putting our trust in the God of healing.

Sam Wells:
I would respond by saying that Jesus sometimes heals but Jesus always saves. The stories that you've told are stories of salvation. You can't have healing without forgiveness; healing without forgiveness is useless. The relationships of trust that are highlighted in Stanley's story are where the truth can be spoken. It's a hard thing to say, but both of you said it in different ways. Actually if you have the forgiveness and if you have the eternal life then there are cases where you don't really need the healing. Russ, you've even said that a healing would have almost taken something away for the community. What your church learned was that forgiveness and eternal life were so great that only one word could describe it: salvation. If you've got salvation, you've actually got the gospel.

To understand the relationship between healing and salvation we need to name precisely what salvation is. It's about past and future. Salvation is the transformation of our past from a burden to a gift—from a place of grief and regret to a heritage of wisdom and joy. And salvation is the transformation of our future from curse to a blessing—from a place of fear and death to a destiny of hope and glory. When we talk about the salvation of the past we call it *the forgiveness of sins*. When we talk about the salvation of the future we call it *eternal life*. These are the gifts Jesus brought in his life, death and resurrection: the forgiveness of sins and eternal life. The restoration of the past and the promise of the future. This is what salvation is.

And so what is healing? Well we know that even when we've been forgiven, there's still a mess to clear up. Forgiveness takes away the guilt and the blame and the enmity and the shame, but it doesn't immediately take away the pain and the loss and the hurt and the damage. Something else is required. And we also know that eternal life may last for ever, but there's some parts of it we'd like right now, because there are parts of ourselves and our lives and our relationships and our communities that are diseased and deathly. Something is required right now—a kind of advance payment of eternal life. And the name we give to those two things, the part that remains to be done when forgiveness has done its work, and the part that we need to be done right now despite our hope for life eternal, is the same name: that name is 'healing'. Healing is the third part of salvation, the part sandwiched between forgiveness and eternal life. This is what salvation means: there's forgiveness, there's eternal life, and in between, filling up any space that may linger between forgiveness and everlasting life, there's healing.

Now what we think we want is healing. What we truly *need* is forgiveness and eternal life. Sometimes we get healing, sometimes we don't. If we get healing in the context of forgiveness in the past and the hope of eternal life in the future, it's a kind of fulfillment of forgiveness and an anticipation of eternal life. If we get healing in the absence of the things we really need, we may find it pretty much useless.

Steve Chalke:
Following on from that, Russ's example reminds me of a story that illustrates how, sometimes, the desire for healing stands in the way of salvation for the whole community. I know of a situation where, some years ago, a leader of a large charismatic church got cancer. The church had that theology that says: 'If you speak something, it comes to be.' So, if we say: 'The cancer won't go away', we're actually buying into negativity and speaking a curse. Therefore God won't be able to heal.'

This theology drove the whole church, many hundreds of people, into denial. They prayed every single day for healing. They prayed, celebrated, received prophetic words of encouragement, and thanked God, but no one was allowed to mention anything about the possibility of death. I was a friend of the man suffering with cancer and for some reason he trusted me, so I'd go to visit him. He wanted to talk about this thing but his church prevented it. When death finally came, no one had ever even had an honest conversation, with him, or anyone else, about parting and death. There was no closure, only unspoken, and unspeakable, questions. In that sense, the desire for healing had stood in the way of salvation.

Sam Wells:
Healing becomes an idol.

Steve Chalke:
That's a common story actually.

Luke Bretherton:
I have a favourite line of Karl Barth: 'Life is not a second God.' That's part of the problem here; these people have made life a second god. That relates to the summary of Augustine's understanding of ethics, sin is people loving right things the wrong way. His ethics are about the disordered nature of our loves and the moral life is about how we should order our love. In these cases, it's not the desire for healing or use of medicine that's wrong, it's about how we order them in relation to loving God. When we love God or love the kingdom first, other things can be put in their proper place.

So, moving on to crime and punishment. Broadly, it's about our ability to negotiate a common life. In a sense, the huge inflation in the number of people in our prisons shows the problems in our common life. But how does the church address crime and punishment? How does it respond to prisoners and what distinctive voice does the church have in this situation?

Stanley Hauerwas:
Let me start by saying I don't like the language of social justice. I don't like the language of restorative justice. I don't like an adjective in front of justice. If it's justice, it's justice. If Jesus is our justice, then mercy is constitutive of justice. My way of putting it is to say that you're not punished for sin; sin is punishment. Punishment is the form of penance for a person to be restored to community. Ex-communication or the ban isn't saying we're throwing you out; it's saying we've discovered that you're out and these are the conditions for coming back. Penance rightly understood is a gesture of the community's love.

Russell Rook:
Can I just ask Stanley to briefly expand upon how sin is its own punishment?

Stanley Hauerwas:
Sin is the punishment because it alienates us from God. It's a kind of loneliness. For example, killing creates a kind of loneliness that makes people unable to communicate what killing another human being has done to them. That's what happens so often with souls. They kill and then have to bear the burden of that terror. To make things worse, we don't give them any ability to confess. The church overcomes the silence and loneliness that sin creates in us. Alienation from God is a punishment, a terrible punishment.

Let's think about capital punishment. It's such a gesture of vengeance, but vengeance is not inhuman. You hear people who've had a child violently murdered and they say: 'I just don't want to live in the same world as the person who has perpetrated this crime.' Symbolically, it's a way of saying that order is deeper than disorder. We have to reply that order is indeed deeper than disorder; order is Jesus. That order shows that even 'that person' is redeemed and is our brother or sister. That helps you see what a radical business this Christianity is.

Luke Bretherton:
There's an analogue here in terms of church life. One of the issues is that we talk about justice and prisons, but in order to learn to talk properly about punishment and crime, we should start with church discipline. How do we talk about crime and punishment in churches and deal with modes of disciplining that aren't coercive and judgemental, but are about re-inclusion. I was wondering whether Stanley could expand on John Howard Yoder's reflections on the ban and the function of the ban.

Stanley Hauerwas:
It's Matthew 18; we simply don't know how to enact this passage. Jesus didn't say: 'If someone has wronged you, you might think about confronting that person.' That's the way we want to read it. On the whole, we prefer to think that they wronged us but we're going to put up with it because we sure as hell don't want to confront them because we might find out they haven't wronged us or that we have to forgive them.

Jesus said: 'If someone has wronged you, you've *got* to go and confront that person.' It's not accidental that this is the central text for the Anabaptists. They understand that peace can only be possible in a community of conflict; you don't let things just simmer until they boil up.

Of course, Matthew 18 is the basis in James for what developed as the penitential rite. We Protestants don't have a penitential rite, so we confess our sin, but we don't have the slightest idea of what we're confessing. We just end up with a generalised sense that: 'I'm crap.' But that doesn't do anybody much good. I would like to see a move back to some kind of proper confessional practice.

Luke Bretherton:
It's also essential to the text that the one who has ruptured the community or ruptured the relationship isn't then

expelled, but becomes as a gentile, i.e., one who is a subject of mission. Your attitude towards them is like someone on your Alpha course, or whatever: you have to reorient your attitude to them. You have to recognise there is a problem to be addressed. We can't just skate over the problem. That's part of the reason our churches collapse, because people ignore the issues and then the relationships collapse.

Sam Wells:
But we need to remember the body of Christ language here. You have to remember that your hand is not with you at the moment and you will not become whole again until your hand is joined onto your arm. It's not the, 'This is going to hurt me more than it hurts you' thing, but a real grief that says: 'We need you back if we are to be whole. We are longing for you to come back. But we are not going to pretend that you have not gone a long way away.'

Shane Claiborne:
Talking about confession and restoration, we had an experience in our community. We talk a lot about the importance of straight talk, talking directly with one another. One time, we had someone living with us who was taking money from the common pool. It kept happening over and over and eventually, people got pretty upset about it. So we had a meeting and in this meeting, we told the person: 'We all know the problem. What do you think should happen?' We asked in a really callous way, almost ignoring any other problems or

issues that might be surrounding this issue. The person broke down said: 'I should just get kicked out. That's what has happened everywhere else I go.'
What was said just floored all of us. I replied: 'We had hoped that we're a little different from all the other places you might go.' All

together, we talked about the money issue and in that moment, the person started sharing about how there were a lot of economic and class dynamics that we hadn't recognized. For instance, if we wanted to go out and get Chinese food, all of us had some sort of income to do that. But since our friend was unemployed, when a chicken wings craving struck, there was no money for chicken wings. There were these subtle disparities in economics and to make things worse, it wasn't necessarily easy to be good when there was money sitting in a mailbox. There were a whole lot of things that we learnt through that.

The most powerful lesson was how to practice the real sacrament of confession. This person was made vulnerable at the moment of confession. The last thing you want to do is beat up people when they're down. In that moment, there was this opposite inertia to pull our community mate back from being broken down and to figure out a solution together. We really felt the importance of making a space for confession and for restoration.

Luke Bretherton:
What you're saying is really important to understanding one of the big hang-ups of the church: judgment versus judgmentalism. People think that either you make no judgement or you're completely judgemental, but you have to make discernments about right and wrong. If this guy is being a schmuck, you need to call him to account, but that doesn't mean you abandon him.

Steve Chalke:
Violent crime is a massive issue in London; how can the church in London speak and live out a judgment on crime without a judgmentalism around those caught up in the web of gang violence? How can we say: 'This is wrong', yet, at the same time create an environment in which transformation is not only possible but probable? I ask this because a kid in our church got stabbed yesterday evening. In the last year, four families in our church in Central London had a relative shot or stabbed to death.

Shane Claiborne:
Something really incredible happened in Longdale, Chicago. Longdale Community Church is in an area of Chicago where there's a lot of street violence going on as well as a lot of police brutality and police misconduct. The church was at a loss about how to deal with the violence.

As they were trying to provide some security for the neighbourhood, they got to know their neighbours by going into the streets. Eventually, they had a recovery community of Hope House men who committed themselves to be on the street all night long. They dressed up in bright, neon tabards and they went out onto the street corners to watch the police and the gangs. The result was unbelievable. The men didn't have any weapons, but they knew everybody on the street. Just having an eye on the street is one way to do it.

Another community connected to us had tons of prostitution in their area. They began to have a rummage sale out on the street everyday so they could meet the people there. The ethos of the street changes when eyes and people are out and visible and able to interact.

Luke Bretherton:
They have the equivalent of that in London, in Manchester, in Birmingham. It's called Street Pastors. They go out on the street, particularly on Saturday and Friday night. They do everything: picking up the girl who's being sick, who's in danger of being raped, and making sure she gets home; stopping fights, intervening early so the situation doesn't escalate.

Stanley Hauerwas:
I have a thought experiment that I've used for many years. When people say that we ought to have capital punishment to deter crime, I tell them that they're exactly right, but that we've got to disassociate capital punishment from the wrong crime. We ought to set up a guillotine on Wall Street and kill people for stock fraud. I was saying this even before Bernie Madoff. People who commit stock fraud cause a lot more harm than your street criminal. The effects of their crime reach so many people and just devastate the victims. So let's take the

stock frauders before the guillotine on Wall Street, televise it; it'd just be great. I bet if we cut off four or five heads we'd really do something to stop fraud on Wall Street.

People said: 'Well, gee, we can't do that.' 'Why?' And they said: 'It doesn't seem commensurate with the crime.' Well, in Texas we've been killing people for horse theft for a long, long time. If you stole someone's horse in the desert, they were dead. People need to think again about the idea that punishment is really deterring something. Do we know what we're doing when we punish?

Luke Bretherton:
Let's move from capital punishment into war and peace.

Steve Chalke:
Well, the big criticism that's always thrown at you if you talk about non-violent responses, peace-making, and turning the other cheek, is: 'If we'd have gone down that route in the Second World War, Europe would be run by Nazis now. Non-violence doesn't work. It's a nice theory, but it doesn't work. In the UK we were redeemed by the Spitfire.'

Sam Wells:
I talk about three kinds of Christian ethics: universal, subversive, and ecclesial [see chapter 2]. Universal is ethics for anyone. Subversive is ethics for the suppressed or the excluded, and ecclesial ethics is for the church. If ethics is fundamentally for the individual, then clearly war is something that can't be handled on an individual level. You need to engage corporately with war and if you spend most of your ethical energy diminishing the church and highlighting the individual, then all you've got left as a corporate entity is the nation state.

Since your ethics deal only with the individual, when

you have to deal with the corporate, you go straight to the level of the nation-state and the 'we' becomes 'we British' or something of that kind. The 'we British' becomes the only 'we' that you can really contemplate.

The problem with the World War II example is when you start the clock. The clock always starts at Munich in that story. The clock never starts with the German Christians embracing Hitler in the early 1930's. And if the Christians hadn't endorsed Hitler, then there would have been no Hitler, and the problem with that is that people think that's irrelevant. We're talking about Britain vs. Germany. My response is: I thought we were talking about what the church should do.

The danger of evangelical ethics is it drifts into universal ethics. It quickly realizes these standards can't be expected from non-Christians and so it stops being *Christian* ethics altogether, in the service of being ethics for anyone. All the distinctive practices of the church get lost that make up ecclesial ethics. Ecclesial ethics fundamentally says: 'We actually can't resolve all these issues unless we use all the things God's given us to resolve them.' We haven't used any of those things that make us distinctive because we believe that our job is to resolve issues for everyone.

If you don't make something like that three-fold distinction, you become very confused about whether the Ten Commandments should be translated into legislation, etc. And I don't think you can resolve any of those issues unless you clear the space of your life to talk about what it would be like to live as peaceful people. You can't start a conversation with people who want to defend the nation-state unless you've got some sense of what's distinctive about Christian practices in the first place. You have to have the conversation that way around.

Luke Bretherton:
What stops Christian ethics, or distinctive moral, Christian practices, from simply becoming ecclesiastical house rules? Is it just a matter of different moments? For example, there are ways of being distinctive as the church. In times of conflict and violence, the particular response that is called forth from

Christians is non-violence. But then, there's another, different moment when we're trying to work out how to negotiate a common life with a whole bunch of other people who aren't necessarily in the church. Is that when we talk about things like just war or do we never talk about things like just war because that would betray our ecclesiastical house rules? Are there different moments in the conversations with different kinds of responses appropriate to who is in the conversation, or are the different moments utterly exclusive?

Sam Wells:
Well, for me, it's always about the imagination. For example, Christian Peace Maker Teams are bursting open our imagination to see the abundance of God in a place where it seems there are only two options: lie down and be trampled on, or take up arms and do the treading. They are a gift to the church because they are breaking open our imagination. This is all about the cross and resurrection, the sacrifice that was finished in AD 33. That was it, the last sacrifice. The resurrection is living in the world made possible by believing that Jesus was the last sacrifice.

Russell Rook:
One of my questions that I wanted to ask in a previous conversation was about something you said Stanley. You said: 'Thou shalt not kill'— end of story. Then you made a comment about how you have tremendous respect for the American military. What did you mean by that?

Stanley Hauerwas:
They are the last honour society

Sam Wells:
The problem is not with the military; they don't declare war. The government declares war.

Stanley Hauerwas:
I don't want Christians in the military but I honour those that are. But there is a problem for advocates of a just war approach with the American military. If you are an advocate of a just war approach you want conscientious participation by soldiers. Most of the people in the American military at below sergeant never knew they had an alternative. So how do you get conscientious participation amongst them? And I say, look, when do you want to start with developing a just war approach? Is the current organization of the Pentagon a just war organization? Is United States foreign policy based on just war? I mean, advocates of just war theory want to sit back and say: 'Oh, we got the seven criteria. Let's see if the war in Iraq gets five out of seven? That's good enough.' Well, the question is why are you in Iraq? You're in Iraq because you had an army left over from the cold war that was so large you could do it. Now, should you have had that large enough army on just war grounds? I'm more than ready to enter into conversation with just war people to discuss what kind of re-organization of our society is needed in order to have a just war foreign policy? Or what kind of re-organization you need to have a just war Pentagon? It's going to be one hell of a lot smaller and you're not going to be all that happy with the current arrangements because what you got is a realist foreign policy and a realist Pentagon which has no moral framework. So don't give me this nonsense that somehow I've withdrawn from direct policy, from real engagement. Just war people have just as much burden as we that are committed to Christian non-violence to say how their policies are realistic.

Luke Bretherton:
But it seems to me that we're talking about a spectrum issue. As I understand it, your position is that you don't oppose the use of force in certain contexts as a police measure. Police action renders the use of force, to defend the innocent, morally licit.

Stanley Hauerwas:
The police function of the state is where just war most determinately works. That's where you get the separation between those that use force and the judgment about the use of force. You don't get that in war. If a war isn't just, then what is it? Just-war isn't about seeing if an ongoing war fits a  certain number of criteria. Instead it asks: 'Are the appropriate limits in place so that we can rightly call this war?'

But the bottom line is, I mean, my kind of slogan thing is to say is, Christians are not called to non-violence because we believe non-violence is a strategy to rid the world of war. Rather, as faithful followers of Christ, we cannot imagine being anything other than non-violence. That may make the world more violent because non-violence, if it's truthful, will challenge those forms of order that call themselves 'peace' but are really based on hidden violence. It's a hard task but I believe we're called to do it.

Sam Wells:
That's the difference between universal and ecclesial ethics in a nutshell.

Steve Chalke:
What did you say about hidden violence disguised as peace? Could you give examples?

Sam Wells:
My favourite one is the cowboy with a Colt 45 called the Peacemaker. It's like having a missile called a Patriot.

Shane Claiborne:
With September 11th, we have a lot to learn from the families that suffered deeply. Many of the families began to mourn together because of their faith and they become a group called Families

for Peaceful Tomorrows. Originally, it was a support group and that's what a lot of people needed. It was someone to be angry with, someone to cry with, someone to ask questions with, and so on, but, as they saw the response of the government, their campaign became: 'Our grief is not a cry for war'.

Many of them went over to Iraq and Afghanistan to be with families there. The stories that they brought back are so redemptive. Families bought them flowers and presents to bring back to New York and D.C. Those are the stories that I think are gospel stories. Maybe they decrease violence, maybe they don't, but regardless, that's the sort of creativity we have to have.

I was there during the invasion of Iraq and one of the lines that I'll never forget came from Baghdad. In the middle of the bombing, bombs were falling everywhere, there were families in the hospital and the manager of the hospital in Baghdad came out crying. He said: 'I haven't slept in 48 hours and all I see is blood.' He threw his hands in the air and said: 'This is from a world that's lost its imagination.'

Endnotes

[1] Edited from a conversation recorded at Duke Divinity School, Durham, NC, USA, 13th August, 2009.

Chapter 9

Sex in Public: How Adventurous Christians Are Doing It

Stanley Hauerwas

On speaking candidly and as a Christian about sex

Candour is always to be striven for, but it is especially important for any discussion about sex; in particular, the morality of sex. And candour compels me to say that I cannot provide anything like an adequate ethic to deal with sex. This is, no doubt, partly because of my own moral and intellectual limitations. But it also reflects the fact that generally Christians, and in particular Christian ethicists, are unsure what to say or how to respond to our culture's changing sexual mores (if in fact they are changing).[1]

Current reflection about sexual ethics by Christian ethicists is a mess. That may seem an odd state of affairs, for it is generally thought that while the church may often be confused about issues of war or politics, we can surely count on Christians to have a clear view about sex. It *has been assumed* that the church and her theologians have seldom spoken ambiguously about sex and most of what they have had to say took the form of a negative.[2] No, you should not have sexual intercourse before marriage. No, you should not commit adultery. No, you should not practice contraception. And so on.

Indeed, the proscriptive nature of much of the church's teaching about sex (together with the assumption often associated with such strictures that there is something wrong with sex), seems to me the source of some of the confusion concerning current sexual ethics. By rights, theologians and ethicists should not be able to say enough good things about sex. Broad anthropological analysis has shown us that we are fundamentally sexual beings, and that is indeed a good thing. God has created us to be sexual beings and it seems nothing short of Manichaean for us to deny that aspect of our lives. But in our rush to show that Christians know that sex can be beautiful, Christian ethicists have often failed to talk candidly about sex. One suspects that if sex can be beautiful, it is as often likely to be messy or boring.

Many people are particularly disturbed when they are told that contemporary Christian ethics has little coherent to say about sexual ethics. We live in a cultural situation that is extremely confusing in regard to sex and we rightly feel we need some guidance from somewhere. Whether we are sexually faithful in our marriages or not, we feel at a loss to explain why we live that way rather than another. Thus, some stay faithful because they are fearful of women or men, or lazy, or fear the consequences if found out. If or how sexual fidelity is anchored in our fundamental Christian convictions remains unclear.[3]

This is an area about which the church and Christian ethicists surely ought to have something to say, but I think what we should have to say will demand a more thorough rethinking of the nature of Christian life than most who call for a new 'sex ethic' anticipate. For it is my thesis that the development of a sexual ethic and practice appropriate to basic Christian convictions must be part of a broader political understanding of the church. Put bluntly, there is no way that the traditional Christian insistence that marriage must be characterized by unitive and procreative ends can be made intelligible unless the political function of marriage in the Christian community is understood.[4] Sexual ethics cannot be separated from political ethics if Christians are to make sense of why sexual practices are to be determined by how they contribute to the good of the Christian community.

Methodologically, this means that attempts to base a Christian ethics of sex on natural law—whether natural law be understood as unexceptionable norms or broadly construed anthropological characterizations of human sexuality—must be abandoned. Ironically, the attempt to develop a sexual ethic based on natural law (i.e. the idea that the legitimacy of contraception can be determined by the nature of the act of sex considered in itself) has much in common with the current effort to liberalize sexual ethics through suggestions about what is necessary for the flourishing of human sexuality.[5] The attempt to base an ethic of sex on 'nature' results in abstracting sex from those institutions that are necessary to make any ethic of sex intelligible. In contrast, I will try to show that the claim that a sexual ethic derives its form from marriage is a political claim, as it makes sense only in terms of the church's understanding of its mission. Therefore, a Christian ethic of sex cannot be an ethic for all people, but only for those who share the purposes of the community gathered by God and the subsequent understanding of marriage.

The thesis that the ethics of sex is a public and political issue seems to be odd or even absurd in our cultural context. We have been taught to understand that sex is private and is determined by two or more people with free consent. It is often assumed that you can do pretty much what you want as long as you do not 'hurt' one another. What we have failed to note is that the claim that sex is a matter of private morality is a political claim dependent upon a liberal political ethos. Any attempt to reclaim an authentic Christian ethic of sex must begin by challenging the assumption that sex is a 'private' matter.

Our current sexual ethics is largely made up of inconsistent borrowings from the various options provided by our culture, because by and large Christians have not lived or understood the political nature of their convictions about marriage and sex. Currently, realism and romanticism seem to be the two main cultural alternatives with regard to how people think about sex. These options appear to be fundamentally opposed, but I think on analysis they share some strikingly similar presuppositions. For realism is but chastened romanticism that seeks to 'talk sense' about sex in order to prevent some of the worst excesses of romanticism. Yet like romanticism, realism continues to underwrite the assumption that sex is a private matter and is subject to public interest only when it has consequences (e.g. teenage pregnancy) that affect the public pocketbook. A brief analysis of realism and romanticism will make evident that they have set the agenda for the current discussion of sexual ethics among Christians.

Realism

As the term suggests, realism has the virtue of dealing with sex without illusion or cant. Realists often claim to be amoral, but that does not mean the realist vision lacks depth. For the realist simply assumes that it is too late to raise 'moral issue' about sex, one way or the other. We live in a situation where two out of ten young girls in New Jersey are going to get pregnant this year. The realist may deplore the implications but assumes the situation as a fact and concentrates on the task of information: how to get knowledge and techniques to young people who have become 'sexually active'[6] so some of the consequences of their behaviour can be checked.

The realist position is also often coupled with an attempt to help people have a more healthy attitude toward sex. In particular, the realists stress that sex is simply one human activity among others—it can be a profound human expression or it can just be fun—but what is important, no matter how sex is understood, is that it be demystified. The realist thus suggests to young people that they may not be as ready for sex as they think they are, for as the sexually experienced often discover, sex is not easy to keep just fun.

Realism is a position I often find myself tempted to assume. I still remember vividly when in 1970, my first year of teaching at the University of Notre Dame, I was asked by a delegation of students from the college's student senate what the 'Christian ethical position' should be concerning whether doors in the dorms could be shut during visiting hours by members of the opposite sex. Completely taken aback by what seemed to be the triviality of the issue, all I could think to say was that I supposed closing the door was better than getting grass stains. My response was meant to be realistic. I assumed that those students who were going to have sex were going to do so whatever rules one thought up about parietals.[7] And like most realists, I thought that the most important thing anyone could do when confronted by such an issue was to speak candidly.

Yet, in spite of the kind of 'worldly wisdom' that makes the realist position attractive, it is doomed to failure. What realists fail to recognize is that, in spite of claims to be amoral or at least nonmoralistic, their position in fact presupposes an ethical recommendation. Realists cannot help but assume that the way things are is the ways things ought to be. In so doing, realists accept as morally normative the liberal assumption that sexual activity should be determined by what each individual feels is good for him or her.

By accepting such an assumption, moreover, realism fails to provide an adequate response to our other primary cultural alternative, romanticism. For many teenagers get pregnant exactly because of their romantic notion that sex should be a significant gesture denoting the level of commitment between two people. In an ironic way the phenomenon of teenage pregnancy, which no doubt is often the result of ignorance and an absence of proper contraceptive techniques, is the sign of how deeply conservative assumptions about the significance of sex are ingrained in our culture.

Romanticism

Like realism, romanticism is less a coherent position than a general stance about the place of sex and marriage in our lives. The basic assumption of romanticism is that love is the necessary condition for sex and marriage. How love is understood can and often does vary greatly among different versions of romanticism. Yet for all romantics, the quality of the interpersonal relation between a couple is the primary issue for considering sexual involvement. Even the arguments that criticize romanticism structurally may accept the assumption that the primary issue is the 'depth' of commitment between the couple.

Examples of this kind of thinking in our society are almost endless, but by way of illustration let me call your attention to the position of Nena and George O'Neill as developed in their best-selling 1972 book, *Open Marriage*.[8] Though I do not think the O'Neills provide a particularly profound version of romanticism, I suspect that they represent broadly shared views and judgments about sex and marriage in our culture.

Ironically, theirs is essentially a conservative position, written in the spirit of saving marriage as a worthwhile activity. To save marriage, however, they argue that the meaning of marriage

> must be independently forged by a man and a woman who have the freedom to find their own reasons for being, and for being together. Marriage must be based on a new openness—an openness to one's self, an openness to another's self, and openness to the world. Only by writing their own open contract can couples achieve the flexibility they need to grow. Open marriage is expanded monogamy, retaining the fulfilling and rewarding aspects of an intimate in-depth relationship with another, yet eliminating the restrictions we were formerly led to believe were an integral part of monogamy.[9]

Open marriages must necessarily avoid being controlled by presupposed roles denoted by the terms 'husband' and 'wife'. What we do and do not do as husbands and wives should be determined by what we feel as individual human beings, not by some predetermined set of restrictive codes.[10] Thus, in an 'open marriage, each gives the other the opportunity, the freedom, to pursue those pleasures he or she wishes to, and the time they do spend together is fruitfully and happily spent in catching up on one another's individual activities.'[11] Crucial to such a marriage is trust, as only trust provides the possibility for a marriage to be a 'dynamic, growing relationship'.[12] But it must be an 'open trust', in contrast to those forms of trust built on dependability and assured predictability. To have open trust 'means believing in your mate's ability and willingness to cherish and respect your honesty and your open communications. Trust is the feeling that no matter what you do or say you are not going to be criticized.'[13] 'Trust then is freedom, the freedom to assume responsibility for your own self first and then to share that human self in love with your partner in a marriage that places no restrictions upon growth, or limits on fulfillment.'[14]

This seems an attractive ideal. After all, who could be against trust? And who would deny the importance of each partner's continuing to develop as his or her own person in and outside marriage? For it is surely true that the strength of any marriage is partly judged by the ability of each partner to rejoice in the friendships of the other. Indeed, such friendships can be seen as necessary for the enrichment of any marriage.

Yet, ironically, the O'Neills' account of 'open marriage' requires a transformation of the self that makes intimate relationships impossible in or outside of marriage. Many conservative critics of proposals like 'open marriage' tend to overlook this element, because all their attention is directed to the sexual implication—namely, that premarital and extramarital sex is not condemned. But that element has long been written into the very structure and nature of romanticism.

What the 'conservative' must recognize is that prior to the issue of whether premarital or extramarital sexual intercourse is wrong is the question of character. What kind of people do you want to encourage? Hidden in the question of 'What ought we to do?' is always the prior question 'What ought we to be?' The most disturbing thing about such proposals as the O'Neills' is the kind of person they wish each of us to be. On analysis, the ideal candidate for an open marriage turns out to be the self-interested individual presupposed and encouraged by our liberal political structure and our capitalist consumer economy.

Perhaps this is best illustrated by calling attention to the O'Neills' discussion of adultery. Of course, the O'Neills see no reason why adultery should be excluded from open marriage. After all, most people 'now recognize sex for what it is: a natural function that should be enjoyed for its own earthy self without hypocrisy.'[15] Indeed, extramarital sexual experiences 'when they are in the context of a meaningful relationship may be rewarding and beneficial to an open marriage.'[16] But the O'Neills do provide a word of caution; they suggest that to have an extramarital affair without first 'developing yourself to the point where you are ready, and your mate is ready, for such a step could be detrimental to the possibility of developing a true open marriage.'[17]

I have thought a lot about this very interesting suggestion, namely, that we develop ourselves to be ready to engage in an extramarital affair. What could that possibly mean? Would it mean that we each date and then come home and compare notes on our experience to see how it makes the other feel? And what would be the object of such a project? Surely it is nothing less than for us to learn to devalue sexual expression between ourselves in order to justify it with other people.

But even more interesting, such training would also require that we learn to control, if not destroy entirely, that primitive emotion called jealousy. What is involved in proposals such as the O'Neills' are extremely profound—yet unrecognized—assumptions about the kind of person each of us ought to be. And the O'Neills are quite explicit about this, as they argue that jealousy is but a learned response determined by cultural attitudes dependent on our assumptions about sexually exclusive monogamy. But such possession of another only

> breeds deep-rooted dependencies, infantile and childish emotions, and insecurities. The more insecure you are, the more you will be jealous. Jealousy, says Abraham Maslow, 'practically always breeds further rejection and deeper insecurity.' And jealousy, like a destructive cancer, breeds more jealousy. It is never, then, a function of love, but of our insecurities and dependencies. It is the fear of loss of love and it destroys that very love. It is detrimental to and a denial of loved one's personal identity. Jealousy is a serious impediment, then, to the development of security and identity, and our closed marriage concepts of possession are directly at fault.[18]

Alas, if only Othello could have had the opportunity to have read *Open Marriage*, the whole messy play could have been avoided.

The irony is that romanticism, which began as an attempt to recapture the power of intimate relation as opposed to the 'formal' or institutionalized relationship implied by marriage, now finds itself recommending the development of people who are actually incapable of sustaining intimate relationships. For intimacy depends on the willingness to give of the self, to place oneself in the hands of another, to be vulnerable, even if that means we may be hurt. Contrary to Maslow, jealousy is the emotion required by our willingness to love another at all. Indeed, I suspect that part of the reason the church has always assumed that marriage is a reality that is prior to love is that genuine love is so capable of destruction that we need a structure to sustain us through the pain and the joy of it. At least one reason for sex being limited to marriage, though it is not a reason sufficient to support an intrinsic relation between sex and marriage, is that marriage provides the context for us to have sex, with its often compromising personal conditions, with the confidence that what the other knows about us will not be used to hurt us. For never are we more vulnerable than when we are naked and making the clumsy gestures necessary to 'make love'.

It is true, of course, that romanticism cannot be defeated simply by calling attention to some of the implications inherent in the O'Neills' argument. Indeed, romanticism has become far too complex a phenomenon for it to be easily characterized or criticized. I am content at this point simply to suggest that the romantic assumption that sexual expression is a 'private' matter in fact masks a profound commitment to the understanding of society and self sponsored by political liberalism. Thus, human relations are increasingly understood in contractual terms and the ideal self becomes the person capable of understanding everything and capable of being hurt by nothing.

The current state of Christian reflection about sexual ethics

I suggested above that current Christian reflection about sexual ethics has been limited to trying to adjudicate among various versions of realism and romanticism in order to establish the 'Christian' ethics of sex. What Christian ethicists have been unable to do is provide an account of sexual ethics that is clearly based on an agenda central to the Christian community's own self-understanding. They have been unable to do so because they have failed to see that any discussion of sex must being with an understanding of how a sexual ethics is rooted in a community's basic political commitments.

As a result sexual ethics, though often very insightful, betrays a fatal abstractness. For example, it is often claimed that it is a mistake to begin reflection about sexual ethics by trying to determine if certain kinds of genital sex are right or wrong. Instead, we must begin by recognizing that sexuality is a matter that involves the 'whole person', or that 'sexuality' so understood must be affirmed as a manifestation of the goodness of God's creation. While all of this is no doubt true, we are not sure how such claims give direction to or help us think better about genital sexual activity. Put bluntly, such analysis does little to help us to answer a teenager who wants to know what is wrong with fooling around before marriage.

The directness of such questions tends to frustrate many ethicists as these questions refer to a specific sort of genital activity. Instead, ethicists prefer to call attention to the importance of the presence of love for wholesome sex. Rather than answering 'Yes' or 'No', we say things like 'The physical expression of one's sexuality with another person ought to be appropriate to the level of loving commitment present in that relationship,'[19] or that any one act of 'genital sexual expression should be evaluated in regard to motivations, intentions, the nature of the act itself, and the consequences of the act, each of these informed and shaped by love.'[20]

For instance, like the O'Neills, James Nelson does not believe that the question of infidelity in marriage can be limited to the issue of adultery, but rather is the rupture of the bonds of 'faithfulness, honesty, trust, and commitment between the spouses.'[21] He therefore thinks we must remain open to the possibility that people can be martially faithful without being sexually exclusive. My difficulty with such arguments is this: How would you ever have any basis to know if you are in fact 'faithful' or not? It is certainly the case that often married people harm one another in more profound ways than by having sex with someone else. But it is also the case that sexual fidelity may be the way we learn to be faithful in other aspects of our lives together. I am aware that some couples may have sustained impressive marriages without the commitment to sexual fidelity, but that is not the issue. The issue is what kind of marriage Christians want to encourage as essential to the purposes of their community. All of which may be true, but is a lot for teenagers in the back seat of a car to remember.

This last comment, whilst rhetorically clear, is in some ways deeply unfair. For no ethic, not even the most conservative, should be judged by its ability to influence the behaviour of teenagers in the back seat of a car. What happens there will often happen irrespective of what 'ethic' has been officially taught. Yet I think in a more profound sense people are right to expect ethicists to be concerned about how their 'ethic' might be understood or misunderstood for providing guidance about our actual sexual conduct.

'What is wrong with a little fooling around?' is a frustrating and direct question. But such questions are necessary to remind us that often our attempts to provide sophisticated and nuanced accounts of sexuality are misleading and perhaps even corrupting for our children. That is not to say that any ethic of sex should be written from the perceptive of only what is good for adolescents or relative to what they are capable of understanding, but I am sure any ethic of sex that does not provide direction for how adolescents should learn to understand and govern their sexual behaviour cannot be sufficient.[22] Perhaps one of the crucial tests for any ethics of sex and sexual behaviour is that we be able to explain it honestly and straightforwardly to our children.

To provide that kind of account for our children, however, requires that we are able to presuppose a community with the practices and convictions that makes such an ethic intelligible. Our children have to see that marriage and having children, and the correlative sexual ethic, are central to the community's political task. For only then can they be offered a vision and an enterprise that might make the disciplining of sex as interesting as its gratification.

One Catholic attempt at sexual ethics

Most current attempts at formulating a Christian ethics of sex
continue to assume the apolitical nature of sexual practice and
ethics. Nowhere is this clearer than in the 1977 study entitled
Human Sexuality, commissioned by the Catholic Theological
Society of America. The romantic ideal clearly dominates the
report, as the authors argue that sexuality must be understood
morally as serving the development of persons by calling them
to constant creativity, that is, to full openness to being, to the
realization of every potential within the personality, to a continued discovery and expression of authentic selfhood.
Procreation is one form of this call to creativity, but by no
means is it the only reason for sexual expression. Sexuality further serves the development of genuine personhood by calling
people to a clearer recognition of their relational nature, of their
absolute need to reach out and embrace others to achieve personal fulfillment.[23] In the light of this 'richer' understanding of
'sexuality' the authors of the *Report* argue that we should abandon the traditional language of 'unitive and procreative' and
instead ask whether acts of sexual intercourse are 'creative and
integrative'. 'Wholesome human sexuality' is that which
should 'foster a creative growth toward integration.'[24]

The authors of the *Report* find it 'woefully inadequate' to
evaluate any human sexual behaviour 'based on an abstract
absolute predetermination of any sexual expressions as intrinsically evil and always immoral.'[25] The fact that they refuse to
find contraception morally unacceptable is not surprising on
such grounds, but they also suggest that while it is hard to see
how adultery could be good for all involved, the 'principle' of
'creative growth toward integration' needs also to be applied
in these cases.[26] Thus, even though some suggest that 'co-mar-
ital sexual relations'—that is, situations that involve sexual
activity with one or more persons beyond the 'primary pair
bond' with the consent or encouragement of the marriage partner—appear to contradict the 'characteristics of wholesome
sexual interrelatedness', empirical data do 'not as yet warrant
any solid conclusions on the effects of such behaviour, particularly from the long-range point of view.'[27]

On the same grounds the report concludes that no moral theologian had yet succeeded in producing convincing proof why in every case sexual intercourse must be reserved to marriage.[28] Yet in no way does this imply an approval of promiscuity, as casual sex 'robs human sexuality of its deepest and richest meaning as an expression of intimacy and love.'[29] In casual sex the sexual act is separated from the deeper intrapersonal meaning necessary if it is to realize its creative and integrative potential. Yet the report is careful to remind us that on many of these questions we still lack the empirical data to make an informed and objective judgment.

On that criterion one might well argue that it is the moral responsibility of Catholics to experiment with 'comarital sexual relations' in the hopes of generating the appropriate data. Or that some take as their moral mission to find forms of extramarital sexual relations that will help us determine if such relations always rob human sexuality of its 'deepest meaning'.

In fairness it should be said that the CTSA report is not always so tentative, as it states clearly that there is no question that bestiality 'renders impossible the realization of the personal meaning of human sexuality.'[30] I question, however, if this is consistent with the *Report's* methodology, as such a summary judgment has all the appearance of the biased judgment of city people who have had little experience with country life. At the very least it seems as though the report could have suggested that in these matters, like other forms of sexuality that seem to these writers unusual, we simply need more 'data' before we can make a summary judgment.

The difficulty with the *Report's* recommendations is not just that the criteria 'creative and integrative' are so abstract we have no idea what they might exclude, but the *Report* ironically continues to assume, like more conservative sexual ethics of the past, that a sexual ethic can be formulated in abstraction from how it contributes to the upbuilding of the political task of the church. The conservative sexual ethics of the past seemed to be harsher as they not only said 'No' more readily, but also seemed to care little for the welfare of persons who were having to live such an ethic. In some ways the conservative was right that a sex ethic was not to be judged by whether it produced integrated persons, but the conservative, as well as the authors of the *Report*, equally fail to understand that the kind of 'person' we should be is a prior question, answered only by the nature of the Christian community.[31]

The public character of sex: marriage as a heroic institution

The recovery of a political vision of marriage and appreciation for the public character of sexuality are conceptually and institutionally interdependent. By calling attention to the public context for sexual behaviour and ethics I am not simply reasserting the traditional concern that sex should only take place in a publicly recognizable institution, though I certainly think that is important, but I am making the stronger claim that any sex ethic is a political ethic.[32] This is particularly true of Christian marriage. The vision of marriage for Christians requires and calls forth an extraordinary polity for the very reason that Christian marriage is such an extraordinary thing.

Whereas most recent theories about sexual ethics are individualistic, since they focus primarily on how persons should deal with their bodies and private actions, William Everett has argued that we must see that sexuality is shaped by humanly created institutions and that this formation works for good as well as for evil. But the question is not whether 'the social formation of our sexuality is good or bad, but whether the institutions in which we live are rightly ordered. An ethics of sex must, therefore, be coordinated with an ethic governing the relations among institutions—familial, economic, ecclesial, and political.'[33]

To illustrate his claim, Everett notes that the development of Christian sexual ethics was not merely a part of the quest for a general social order.

> While Augustine was laying the theological basis for a familist social order, counter-currents were also developing to avoid submerging the Church in that order. As the Church was increasingly drawn into the orbits of the princes, a sexual ethic

had to be evolved to separate it from the family-based power of the princes. In the wake of Hildebrand (Gregory VII), celibacy finally became mandatory for clergy in order to separate the Church from the hereditary powers of the princes. Celibacy was as important to the Church's integrity in a familistic social order as constitutional separation of Church and state has become under nationalism. The Augustinian accommodation required a Hildebrandine distance. Celibacy was and is an institutional policy evolved for the sake of the institution. Moreover, this policy had a legitimate purpose—to enable the Church to carry out its mission as a critical and prophetic agent in human affairs.[34]

The church's restraints on various forms of sexual activity were intelligible only to the extent that the church could be a 'counterfamily' to the princes. But, as Everett points out, in our time, when family order is no longer the model of societal order or authority, 'it becomes very difficult to transfer this self-restraint in order to conform to the demands of other institutions.'[35] The family, having lost its political, social, and economic functions, apart from being a unit of consumption, is only intelligible as the context that provides for 'creative integration' through intimate relationship. Thus increasingly the family becomes understood as a voluntary society justified by its ability to contribute to the personal enhancement of each of its members.[36] Everett is not surprised that such an accommodation has occurred, but he wonders if the correlative understanding of sexuality, as that which functions primarily within the private sphere of emotional and ego-related needs, is sufficient to provide a prophetic perspective on our society. For he claims:

> It is not enough to see the pressures of advertising and bureaucratic life as a natural given, for behind these immediate forces like the needs of a capital-intensive economy seeking to maintain a high level of consumption for essentially useless products. It is not enough, therefore, to invoke [as *Human Sexuality* does] 'social responsibility' or 'the common good' as a consideration in sexual decisions, without a more critical analysis of the nature of that society and its conception of the good. We need to be able

to see how the pursuit of 'creative integration' in our bedrooms might depend on the sacrifices of primary-producing nations to the south of us who keep our economy fueled with metals and oil. We need to see how the pleasures and disciplines of mobile individuality are tied to the expressways and housing developments devouring our agricultural land.

The capacity to see those connections is essential to any kind of prophetic or biblical ethic of sex. Not to see the whole is to be victimized by the parts. The CTSA study has comforted those who have adapted to the dominant North American patterns, but it does little to challenge that society or to support those left on the margins. It has met the demands of realistic accommodations but has not gone far enough to provide Christian distance. We have yet to move, in our own time, from Augustine to Hildebrand.[37]

Everett maintains that the development of such a critical ethic awaits an adequate ecclesiology. The ecclesiology of most of the more liberal sexual ethics assumes that the church is a voluntary association that exists for the spiritual enrichment of the individuals composing it. While admitting that such a voluntaristic theory of church is inextricably bound up with a pluralist social context, Everett doubts that voluntarism can provide the countervailing power we need to counter the tremendous powers that shape and often destroy our lives.[38]

Following Everett, I believe that we cannot expect to begin to develop an adequate Christian sexual ethic without starting with the insistence that sex is a public matter for the Christian community. For our sexual ethic is part and parcel of our political ethic. How we order and form our lives sexually cannot be separated from the necessity of the church to chart an alternative to our culture's dominant assumptions. Indeed, it is my contention that Christian conviction concerning the place of singleness and the family is perhaps the most important political task of the church in our society.

Sex and the church's mission

The political nature of the church's sexual ethic is perhaps most clearly illuminated by calling attention to the alternative of singleness as a legitimate form of life among Christians. Indeed, in the strongest possible language the basis and intelligibility of the Christian understanding of marriage makes sense only in relation to the early Church's legitimation for some of 'singleness'.[39] This is often forgotten, as the church is prone, for apologetic reasons, to simply underwrite the broad assumption that marriage is a natural and primary context in which to 'locate' sex. Thus most Christians assume that marriage is the first mode of sexual life and that the single therefore must justify his or her mode of life rather than vice versa. But Christian marriage is not a 'natural' institution but rather the creation of a people who marry for very definite purposes. The constant institutional reminder of this fact is the assumption of the early Christians that singleness was as legitimate a form of life as marriage.

It is worth pointing out that the New Testament seems to have little to say about sex and marriage. And what it does say has a singularly foreign sound for those of us brought up on romantic notions of marriage and sex. We are thus struck by the stark realism of the Pauline recommendations in 1 Corinthians 7 and more than a little embarrassed by the *Haustafeln* [household rules] passages in Ephesians, Colossians, and 1 Peter.[40] As a means to soften these passages, many call attention to 1 Corinthians 13 and Ephesians 5:21–33 to stress that love really is crucial to Christian marriage. Yet this attempt to rescue the New Testament views on marriage and sexuality seem to involve creative forms of exegesis. I am particularly struck by the supposition that Ephesians 5:22ff can be used to justify the importance of 'happy' marriages for Christians. There seems to be nothing in the text itself to suggest that Christ's love and unity with the church implies that unity is without discord.[41]

More important, however, than the interpretation of particular New Testament texts about marriage and sex is the recognition that the church's sexual ethic cannot be determined through examination and collation of individual texts. Of course, the individual texts are significant for helping us understand the early church's sexual ethic, but they must be understood in the broader context of the early Christians' understanding of their mission. Ironically, in that respect singleness is a better indication than marriage of the church's self-understanding.

The early church's legitimation of singleness as a form of life symbolized the necessity of the church to grow through witness and conversion. Singleness was legitimate, not because sex was thought to be a particularly questionable activity, but because the mission of the church was such that 'between the times' the church required those who were capable of complete service to the kingdom. And we must remember that the 'sacrifice' made by the single is not that of 'giving up sex', but the much more significant sacrifice of giving up heirs. There can be no more radical act than this, as it is the clearest institutional expression that one's future is not guaranteed by the family, but by the church. The church, the harbinger of the kingdom of God, is now the source of our primary loyalty.[42]

Extraordinary moral commitments are involved in a community that encourages us to form particular attachments that are morally legitimated to override concern for the general welfare of the community. Christians have legitimated such commitments because they believe that the 'good' that constitutes the church is served only by our learning to love and serve our neighbours as we find them in our mates and children. The sexual exclusiveness traditionally associated with the Christian understanding of marriage is but a form of the church's commitment to support exclusive relationships.

In this respect there is a certain tension in the church's sponsoring of singleness and marriage as equally valid modes of life. But both singleness and marriage are necessary symbolic institutions for the constitution of the church's life as the historic institution that witnesses to God's kingdom. Neither can be valid without the other.[43] If singleness is a symbol of the church's confidence in God's power to affect lives for the growth of the church, marriage and procreation are the symbols of the church's understanding that the struggle will be long and arduous. For Christians do not place their hope in their children, but rather their children are a sign of their hope, in spite of the considerable evidence to the contrary, that God has not abandoned this world. Because we have confidence in

God, we find the confidence in ourselves to bring new life into this world, even though we cannot be assured that our children will share our mission.[44] For they too must be converted if they are to be followers of the way.

From this perspective marriage (as well as the family) stands as one of the central institutions of the political reality of the church, for it is a sign of our faithfulness to God's kingdom come through the providential ordering of history. By our faithfulness to *one* other, within a community that requires, finally, loyalty to God, we experience and witness to the first fruits of the new creation. Our commitment to exclusive relations witnesses to God's pledge to his people, Israel and the church, that through his exclusive commitment to them, all people will be brought into the kingdom.

Marriage as a heroic role

Marriage so understood is a heroic task that can be accomplished only by people who have developed the virtues and character necessary for such a task. The development of such virtues and character is a correlative of a narrative that helps us understand the struggle in which we are involved. But is it exactly such a narrative that we have been lacking, or, perhaps more accurately, our primary problem is that our experience of marriage has been captured by narratives that have done little for, and have perhaps even perverted, the role of marriage in the Christian community.

Contrary to the romanticism so prevalent in our culture, Rosemary Haughton has argued for a 'heroic' view of marriage. Marriage is heroic for Christians because 'the couple must dedicate themselves, not simply to each other, but to work together at something greater than I imagine.'[45] Haughton is not suggesting that such an understanding of marriage will necessarily produce a 'better' marriage than the romantic ideal, but rather that the 'criteria' of success are simply different. 'The point is that the qualities that make people stick out a hard life together, not stopping too much to wonder if they are fulfilled, are the qualities people need if they are to develop the hero in marriage, which is what being married "in the Lord" is about.'[46]

There is one particular quality Haughton finds especially important for the hero: fidelity. The virtue of fidelity is often ignored or attacked by advocates of the romantic model, as romantic love seeks intensity, not continuity. And fidelity seems to contradict the fact that people develop and change, and in doing so it seems unjust that they should remain attached to past commitments. But, as I suggested above, such fidelity makes sense only if it occurs in a community that has a mission in which marriage serves a central political purpose. And marriage has such a purpose for Christians, as it is a sign that we are a community sustained by hope. Marriage is a sign and source of such hope, 'for as long as there are people loving and working together, and bringing up children, there is a chance of new life. To take conscious hold on that life, to realize oneself at the heart of it, for others also, is a tremendously vitalizing spiritual experience.'[47]

Practical implications

'Vitalizing spiritual experience' seems a long way away from answering the query concerning what is wrong with messing around a little before or during marriage. Moreover, there is the added problem that whether the argument above is right or not seems of little relevance to our concrete experience. For the truth of the matter is that few of us had that understanding of what we were doing when we got married; nor has our sexual conduct been formed by or lived out in such terms. As a result, most of what has been said may seem but one more idealistic account of marriage and sex that should properly be dismissed by those of us who have to live in this life.

Yet I think any argument, incomplete as it is, at least provides some means of response. While few of us have been trained to view our marriage in the adventurous ways described above, the perspective I have developed should at least help us deal with the fact that even though we may not have known what we were doing when we got married, we find ourselves married. The important issue is how we are to understand what has happened through marriage. Surely it is not just that we have undervalued or overvalued the significance of sex in our lives, but that we have had no sense that this way of understanding sex represents a destructive alternative.

From the perspective I have tried to develop we can now see why realism is insufficient to provide us with ethical guidance about sex. For realism, as I have argued, turns out to be but a chastened form of romanticism that continues to reflect a culture that insists that sex and marriage have no public function. A true realism requires a community that forms our loyalties in such a manner that both the costs and hopes of marriage can be properly help in balance. Only from such a perspective can we reach a more profound sense of the relation of love and marriage, as it is only within such a context that we can begin to understand that the love properly characteristic of marriage is not a correlative of the attractive qualities of our mates. Only a love so formed has the capacity to allow the other freedom to be other without resentment.[48]

I think also that the account I have tried to sketch out helps explain aspects of our lives that are simply anomalous given our culture's understanding of marriage and the family. I am thinking of such common matters as our deep commitment to our particular children and their care, or of the extraordinary efforts some couples go through to save their marriages, or why we continue to care about having children at all. To be sure, many are finding that it is possible to train ourselves not to have such 'irrational' desires, but there is the lingering feeling that we are poorer for it. Sadder still is that many spouses who remain committed in the midst of difficult marriages and continue caring for children in very difficult circumstances are only able to explain these commitments as expression of their own peculiar desires. It is as if such commitments were merely a matter of taste.

What we forget is that such 'peculiar desires' are the product of centuries of Christian insistence and training that the family is central to what the church means in this time between the times. To be sure, the church often forgets its own best insights and justifies its practice on grounds that appear more amenable or 'natural' to its cultural context, but it continues to have the advantage of having to deal with the necessity of men and women struggling to figure out what they are doing by being married 'in the Lord.' Such a 'necessity' means that the church can never forget for long that marriage among Christians involves commitments not readily recognized by the world.

But I think the perspective I have tried to develop does more than simply help us to interpret our past. It also helps us ask the right question for giving direction to our future. For the issue is not where X or Y form of sexual activity is right or wrong, as if such activity could be separated from a whole way of life. Rather, such questions are but shorthand ways of asking what kind of people we should be to be capable of supporting the mission of the church. The question of sexual conduct before marriage is thus a question of the kind of preparation necessary so that we may well play the roles and perform the tasks that we are called to by the Christian community. It is through coming to understand the roles and tasks to which we are called by God that we learn whether we may be called to a life of singleness or marriage.[49]

The issue is not whether someone is chaste in the sense of not engaging in genital activity, but whether we have lived in a manner that allows us to bring a history with us that contributes to the common history we may be called upon to develop with one another. Chastity, we forget, is not a state but a form of the virtue of faithfulness that is necessary for all who wish to serve a role in the community.[50] As such, it is as crucial to the married life as it is to the single life.

Of course, we need to remind ourselves again, that is still quite a bit to remember in the back seat of a car. But, as I suggested, there is no 'ethic' that in itself can solve all the problems involved in such behaviour. Rather, what the young properly demand is an account of life and the initiation into a community that makes intelligible why their interest in sex should be subordinated to other interests.[51] What they, and we, demand is the lure of an adventure that captures the imagination sufficiently that for Christians 'conquest' comes to mean something other than the sexual possession of another. I have tried to suggest that marriage and singleness for Christians should represent just such an 'adventurous conquest,' which provides us with the skills necessary to know when, how, and with whom to have sex in public.

Endnotes

[1] Indeed, I suspect that the 'crisis' concerning sexual behaviour in our society is not what people are actually doing or not doing, but that we have no way to explain to ourselves or to others *why* it is that we are doing one thing rather than another. Thus, people simply do not know why they do or do not have sexual intercourse before marriage, or even more disturbing, why they should or should not get married at all, or why they should or should not have children. In the absence of any such accounts, pragmatic considerations, which are often filled with wisdom and much good sense, rule the day. However, pragmatic reflection is not sufficient to guide our lives in a manner that helps us have a sense of worth necessary to sustain our own and our community's moral projects.

[2] For an excellent brief overview of the historical development of sexual ethics, see Margaret Farley, 'Sexual Ethics,' *Encyclopedia of Bioethics* (New York: Free Press, 1978), 4:1575–89.

[3] Even more disturbing is what appears to be the sheer sexual anarchy characteristic of much of our culture. For example, Paul Ramsey in a recent article cites Dr. Robert Johnson, director of adolescent medicine at the New Jersey College of Medicine, that two of every ten girls in junior and senior high school in New Jersey will get pregnant this year (see Paul Ramsey, 'Do You Know Where Your Children Are?', *Theology Today* 26, no. 1 [April 1979]: 10-22. No matter what one thinks about premarital sexuality, that is a shocking statistic, and we feel we need some ethical guidance on how to deal with such problems.

[4] [Hauerwas's reference to the unitive and procreative ends of marriage show him in conversation with the Catholic tradition. For an example of the Catholic understanding of the ends of marriage, see the Vatican II document *Gaudium et Spes* (*Pastoral Constitution on the Church in the Modern World*), sections 47–52.]

[5] [The natural law understandings of sex that Hauerwas has in mind are (a) readings of Pope Pius XI's encyclical *Casti Connubii* (1930) and (b) Kosnik et al., *Human Sexuality* (1977).]

[6] Of course, the very phrase 'sexually active' already embodies realist assumptions, since it tries to describe what many assume is a

serious moral issue in morally neutral language. And of course, the 'realist' may be right that such language is more appropriate because it avoids the 'moralistic' language of the past, but it must be recognized that this kind of language-transforming proposal assumes substantive moral presuppositions.

7   Parietels: A set of rules at the University of Notre Dame and some other institutes of higher education dictating visiting hours for the opposite sex in the single sex dorms.

8   Nena and George O'Neill, *Open Marriage* (New York: Avon Press, 1972).

9   O'Neill and O'Neill, *Open Marriage*, 41.

10   O'Neill and O'Neill, *Open Marriage*, 148.

11   O'Neill and O'Neill, *Open Marriage*, 188.

12   O'Neill and O'Neill, *Open Marriage*, 224.

13   O'Neill and O'Neill, *Open Marriage*, 231.

14   O'Neill and O'Neill, *Open Marriage*, 235.

15   O'Neill and O'Neill, *Open Marriage*, 247.

16   O'Neill and O'Neill, *Open Marriage*, 254.

17   O'Neill and O'Neill, *Open Marriage*, 254.

18   O'Neill and O'Neill, *Open Marriage*, 237.

19   James Nelson, *Embodiment* (Minneapolis: Augsburg, 1978), 127.

20   Ibid. Again, the difficulty with such 'criteria' is that one has no idea what would count for or against whether certain forms of activity should be considered shaped by love.

21   Ibid.

22   I owe this point to Anne Harley Hauerwas.

23   Anthony Kosnik et al., *Human Sexuality* (New York: Paulist Press, 1977), 85. It should be noted that though their report was published by the Catholic Theological Society of America the board of that society took pains to make clear that this action implied neither approval nor disapproval of the report.

24   Kosnik et al., *Human Sexuality*, 86.

25   Kosnik et al., *Human Sexuality*, 89.

26   Kosnik et al., *Human Sexuality*, 148.

27   Kosnik et al., *Human Sexuality*, 149.

28   Kosnik et al., *Human Sexuality*, 158.

29   Kosnik et al., *Human Sexuality*, 164.

30   Kosnik et al., *Human Sexuality*, 230.

31   It is, of course, true that *Human Sexuality* does not represent the general consensus of Catholic attitudes about the morality of sexual conduct. But I suspect what it does accurately represent is the confusion of Catholic thought about sex—not just judgments

about particular forms of sexual expression, but confusion about where one should even begin thinking about the ethics of sex. For once the connection between sexual intercourse and procreation is broken, and it has been broken in theory and practice for many Catholics, then it is by no means clear what basis you have for maintaining other judgments about the rightness or wrongness of certain forms of sexual expression. No amount of rethinking of natural law will be able to show that every act of sexual intercourse must be procreative; rather, what must be recaptured is that the connection between the unitive and procreative ends of marriage is integral to the Christian understanding of the political significance of marriage.

32 For a more extensive analysis of this point, see my 'Sex and Politics: Bertrand Russell and "Human Sexuality",' *Christian Century 95*, no. 14 (April 19, 1978), 417–22. The church's traditional condemnation of 'secret marriages' involves substantive assumptions that can be too easily overlooked. For the significance of maintaining that sex should occur in publicly sanctioned contexts (which might well include 'engagements') suggests that we should not trust our declaration of love unless we are willing to commit ourselves publicly. For there is surely no area where we are more liable to self-deception than in those contexts where love is mixed with sexual desire. Of course, there is nothing wrong with love or sexual desire except that we may often confuse the two. The problem with the suggestion that sexual expression should be relative to the level of loving commitment is that it is simply too hard to test the latter. I would suggest instead that the form and extent of our sexual expression is best correlated to the extent we are willing to intermix our finances. It may sound terribly unromantic, but I am convinced that one of the best tests of 'love' is the extent to which a couple are willing to share a common economic destiny. As John Howard Yoder has suggested, 'The ethical question is not whether the sex-with-true-love is by definition sinful, but whether true love can be honest, can be true love if it dodges the honest outward expressions which are its normal social form . . . Therefore what is questionable about 'premarital sex' is not that it is sex, nor that it is pre-marital, but that the maintenance of secrecy, the avoidance of legality, the postponement of common residence and finances, the withholding of public pledge, constitute both a handicap for the marriage's success and *prima facie* evidence that the love is not true. This is not sex-without-marriage but marriage without honesty. It is not that

the hasty youngsters sin against backward cultural mores while fulfilling themselves and consummating their own love: it is that they sin against themselves, their lives, and their marriage, by depriving their love of the *social consummative*, the orderly cohabitative, the fresh air, without which it is stunted or amputated' ('When Is a Marriage Not a Marriage,' unpublished manuscript, 12).

[33] William Everett, 'Between Augustine and Hildebrand: A Critical Response to Human Sexuality,' *Proceedings of the Catholic Theological Society of America 33* (1978), 78.

[34] Everett, 'Between Augustine and Hildebrand', 79.

[35] Everett, 'Between Augustine and Hildebrand', 79. Indeed, the church's shift to 'personalist' accounts of marriage and sexual conduct is an attempt to baptize the transformation of the family occasioned by a capital-intensive economy that needs fewer but better trained workers.

[36] See, for example, Christopher Lasch's account of the effect of liberalism on the family in *Haven in a Heartless World* (New York: Basic Books, 1977).

[37] Everett, 'Between Augustine and Hildebrand', 82.

[38] Even granting that God's hand is at work in the dialectic among these massive institutions, can a purely voluntaristic vision of Christian life provide an adequate ecclesiology that relates our sexuality to our society? Is that kind of community enough to protect our fragile psyches from these potent cultural forces? I think not. A sexual ethic that doesn't place the dilemmas of sexuality in this kind of social context will never reach 'the Hildebrandine moment' (Everett, 'Between Augustine and Hildebrand', 83).

Having said this, I disagree with particular points of Everett's position. In particular, I think that Everett is incorrect in implying that the only way the church challenged the empire was through celibacy. It is extremely important to recognize that the kind of family the church stated to create from the beginning was a means to gain a critical edge against its wider society.

Moreover, even though Everett is right to suggest that no church, not even 'the Catholic church, in our current pluralist context can provide a total ritual environment in which people grow up with their sexual activities already integrated into the symbolism of Church and family' (Everett, 'Between Augustine and Hildebrand', 83), I suspect that a more normative form of sectarianism will be required if we have any hope of articulating and institutionalizing a form of sexual life appropriate to Christians.

Having said this, the structure of Everett's argument seems to me to be right.

39 I am using the locution 'singleness' rather than celibacy, as it is by no means clear that they are the same. Celibacy denotes a life-long vocation, while 'singleness' may be a form of life assumed for a while without excluding the possibility of marriage. While both may be sexually celibate, the rationale for their celibacy is not necessarily of the same order. For an extremely insightful article on singleness that criticizes the church's limitation of the category to the religious, see Mary Jo Weaver, 'Singleness and the Family', *Commonweal* (October 26, 1979), 588–91.

40 For an extremely interesting interpretation of the *Haustafeln*, see John Howard Yoder, *The Politics of Jesus* (Grand Rapids, MI: Eerdmans, 1972), 163–92.

41 Many interpret Ephesians 5:21–33 to mean that marriage is a paradigm of the unity of Christ and his church, but in the passage itself the analogy works the other way, as the relationship between Christ and his church is the paradigm for marriage.

42 And, of course, such loyalty involves the gravest dangers, as was tragically displayed at Jonestown. Jones was right that Christianity in some fundamental ways challenges how we 'naturally' think about the family. His 'solution' to the problem of the family in Christianity reveals the depth of apostasy his peculiar account of Christianity involved, but Jonestown helps us understand what extraordinary assumptions were involved in the early Christian's commitment to marriage and the family. For they too knew they were involved in a revolutionary struggle, yet they continued to sponsor particular commitments and the having of children who were the responsibility of particular parents. For a fuller development of this point, see my 'Self-Sacrifice as Demonic: A Theological Response to Jonestown,' in *Violence and Religious Commitment*, ed. Ken Levi (University Park: Penn State University Press, 1982), 152–62, 189–91.

43 Donald Goergen argues this well in *The Sexual Celibate* (New York: Seabury Press, 1975), 107.

44 It must be remembered that for Christians parenting is not simply a biological role, but an office in a community that everyone in the church shares to some extent. That biological parents bear a particular responsibility for the rearing of children is but one of the ways Christians are reminded of how deeply we are anchored in 'nature', and it manifests the church's stake in exclusive commitments.

[45] Rosemary Haughton, 'Marriage: An Old, New Fairy Tale', in *A Curious Tradition: Marriage among Christians*, ed. James Burtchaell, C.S.C. (Notre Dame, IN: Ave Maria Press, 1977), 142.

[46] Haughton, 'Marriage: An Old, New Fairy Tale', 143. Traditionally all that marrying 'in the Lord' means was simply that Christians should marry other Christians. See, for example, the discussion by E. Schillebeeckx in *Marriage: Secular Reality and Saving Mystery* (London: Sheed and Ward, 1956), 192-202. Schillebeeckx rightly emphasizes that the early Christians did not think they were 'spiritualizing' marriage, but rather than their Christian commitment gave marriage a new intentionality. Thus, Christian marriage did not happen in spite of the human institution of marriage, but in it. That does not mean that Christian marriage can be justified because it involves some special magic that ensures domestic bliss and happiness. Rather, Christian marriage is justified because it is what Christians are called to do for the building up of the community of the faithful.

[47] 'Marriage: An Old, New Fairy Tale', 150.

[48] Christians have far too readily underwritten the romantic assumption that people 'fall' into love and then get married. We would be much better advised to suggest that love does not create marriage; rather, marriage provides a good training ground to teach us what love involves. Indeed, one of the assumptions that Christians should challenge is the general belief that love is an intrinsic aspect of 'natural' marriage. There is simply no good reason to think that, as many cultures provide very acceptable forms of marriage without requiring the couple to 'love' one another. The relation between love and marriage is not necessarily peculiar to Christians, though I suspect the kind of love characteristic of Christian marriage has distinctive aspects. Moreover, I think we should be hesitant to identify this distinctiveness with 'self-sacrifice', as no marriage can long survive as a truth relation built on 'self-sacrifice'. Rather, the distinctiveness of love between Christians must rest on the fact that they share a commitment in common that provides the basis not to fear the truth about themselves or their relation.

It has been suggested to me that my positing of Hauerwas's Law, 'You always marry the wrong person', though meant to challenge romanticism, presupposes romanticism. That may be, but the deeper intent of the 'law' is to suggest that marriage among Christians requires an account that allows us to form a life together where fidelity and love are required without assuming 'common interests'. We learn to love the other not because they are like us but because they are not. See, for example, my 'Love and Marriage,' *The Cresset 40*, no. 8 (June 1977): 20–21.

49 There are many roles in the church, but the roles of singleness and marriage are particularly fundamental, since they derive immediately from what the community is about. However, we must remember that 'singleness' is not ultimately justified because of the requirements of certain tasks or functions, but because it is symbolically crucial to the church's understanding of itself as an eschatological community.

50 Goergen, *The Sexual Celibate*, 98–99.

51 I suspect that part of the current difficulty of developing a sexual ethic for young people is the absence of any other signs and rituals for becoming an adult. Thus, sexual experimentation and/or involvement become the signs in the youth subculture that one has 'grown up'. Of course, rituals of initiation into adulthood only make sense when being an adult involves special privileges and responsibilities because of the tasks it requires.

Chapter 10

How to Die (Rom. 8.28–39)

Samuel Wells

A Sermon preached in Duke University Chapel on August 3, 2008

Woody Allen once said, 'I don't want to achieve immortality through my work . . . I want to achieve it through not dying.' Not long ago I sat by the bedside of a man who felt just the same way. He knew he had just a few days to live. 'I want to do something for my wife and my children,' he said, 'And maybe for my friends as well. I can't think of anything I can give them now, stuck here in this bed.' I said to him, 'Have you ever thought that you're more than capable of giving them one of the most precious gifts anyone could give, a gift all the more precious because it's so rare?' 'What gift might that be?' he said. I waited to see if he would look at his circumstances and guess for himself, but after some moments of silence, I said, 'A good death.'

What is a good death? A good death is a window into the glory of God. A good death is a revelation of Paul's conviction that 'nothing can separate us from the love of God in Christ Jesus our Lord.' The reality of modern medicine is that relatively few of us will be fully conscious, lucid, and full of parting wisdom, up to the very moment of our deaths. As one person said, 'On the plus side, death is one of the few things that can be done just as easily lying down.' The various tubes and machines will more often than not keep us technically going for some period of time after our last conscious thought or word. So we need to start getting our plans in order now, ahead of time, if we intend to give our families, friends, and society the gift of a good death. Preparing us for a good death forces us to live a good life. The less you can do about the length of your life, the more you need to attend to its breadth and depth.

We probably all know people who are either so worried about the *future* or so angry or regretful or otherwise burdened about the *past* that they seem to spend little or none of their lives in the *present* tense. The first thing to hope for as we approach the reality of death is to find or receive the grace to be *present*, to live in the present tense. Finding the ability to live in the present is very similar to what many people call being 'at peace'. To live in the present tense and be at peace in the face of death requires two things.

(1) It requires us to believe that the past is taken care of. This is fundamentally a matter of coming to terms with our humanity. Few if any of us can honestly say our lives turned out as we had hoped or expected. It's easy, perhaps natural, to apportion blame for that. (a) If grievances and resentments are heavy on our heart and the gift of forgiveness hasn't accompanied a long journey of healing, it can be easy to blame others for everything. (b) But we can just as easily blame ourselves. For a great many people, the difficulty of accepting forgiveness is at least as much of an obstacle to a good death as the difficulty of offering forgiveness. (c) Yet we can also blame Life, or God, whichever we choose to call it, for the quirks of science or nature or the economy or history, that made our life less than we would have liked it to be. In the words of one rueful commentator, 'Life is full of misery, loneliness, and suffering—and it's all over much too soon.' Whether mocked or praised by others, whether starting from great privilege and prospects or from lowly fortune and station, whether littered with accolades and achievements or with setbacks and shame, so many of us regard our lives as more or less a failure.

In all these ways looking back on the past is coming to terms with our humanity, with the humanity of those around us, and with the limitations and weaknesses of the human spirit. Life

and death are both about coming to terms with these limitations, and for the person who has learned to live with others,
with themselves, and with the contingency of circumstances,
we have a word: we call that person patient.

(2) I said that living in the present tense requires two things,
and we discovered that the first one is to believe the past is
taken care of. The second one, which might seem even more
pressing in the face of death, is to believe the future is taken
care of. If letting go of the past is fundamentally about coming
to terms with our humanity, opening our lives wholehearted-
ly to the future is fundamentally about coming to terms with
God's divinity. Now the future is unknown. For many, perhaps
most, people the unknown that lies beyond the threshold of
death is simply the most terrifying thing in all human comprehension, precisely because it defies human comprehension.
I'm going to attempt briefly to break that terror down into its
constituent elements, to make it easier to talk about.

(a) For some people the big fear beyond death is judgement.
For most of Christian history this has been what Christianity
was really all about—preparing you to face the finality of
judgement, and its bifurcation between heaven and hell. It's
amazing how this has become so much less of an issue to
people in the last 150 years, and consequently how attention
has focused so much more on the conditions and possibilities
and desire for justice in this present life. Nonetheless, the fear
of hell weighs heavy on many of us as we approach death.
While we may not imagine perpetual fire or gnashing of teeth,
it's not hard to imagine being alone for ever, a very gloomy
prospect. And if one adds to that the possibility of everlasting
pain, whether due to punishment or some other reason connected to the continuation in some form of our sense experience, it's too much to bear to think about.

(b) Perhaps the biggest fear for the contemporary imagination, captivated as most of us are by the realization and fulfil-
ment of the individual self, is that beyond death lies simply
oblivion. It is rationally hard to square the myriad complexity
and texture of human existence before death with total empti-
ness afterwards. But when we witness the mundane biological
process of death in animals and plants, there can seem little

observational reason to argue that humans will be significantly different. As Johnny Carson famously said, 'For three days after death hair and fingernails continue to grow but phone calls taper off.' We're left with just our bodies and the worms. All the restorative qualities of sleep suddenly go out the window, and we are faced with a sleep without end, a complete annihilation of the self—for many, perhaps most of us, a horrifying prospect.

When St. Paul is writing the stirring words which conclude the eighth chapter of his letter to the Romans, he is addressing precisely these overwhelming fears—the fear of judgement, or at least of being eternally alone or perpetually in pain, and the fear of oblivion, of one's consciousness being wiped out of the drama of existence. He is telling his readers, 'Each one of you is precious in God's sight. You are not merely biological human products. You are known, loved, called, redeemed, chosen. And you will be glorified. A whole set of forces may be against you—hostile others, troubling and extreme circumstances, even yourself: but if God is on your side, none of these will overcome you—indeed *you* will overcome *them*, with something to spare. No power, nothing in the past, nothing in the future, no biological necessity, no demise of human cells, no amount of pain, and no sense of isolation will separate you from the love of God in Christ Jesus.

So in the face of our fear of *judgement*, the good news is that God in Christ is *for* us. This is what we discover in Jesus' healing ministry in Galilee and what we see when Jesus takes God and the world's punishment on our behalf on Golgotha. And in the face of *oblivion* the good news is that God in Christ is *with* us. This is what we realize is God's earthly purpose when Jesus comes among us as a baby at Christmas and what we discover is God's eternal purpose when Jesus returns to us as our risen Lord at Easter. God is *for* us and God is *with* us. This is the essence of the good news of Christ.

To bring these claims back to our mundane and needy emotional experience, our biggest fears about those we love are that either they will come to hate us or they will forget about us. St. Paul is telling us that in our eternal relationship with God neither of these eventualities is possible. God *cannot* turn against us and God *cannot* forget about us. Because of Jesus we will remain perpetually at the forefront of God's heart and mind. This is the gospel. This is the good news about the future that enables us to see our lives through to a good death. That doesn't mean we don't still have fears about judgement and oblivion. The point about the assurance of Paul's words is that they enable us to face the future *in spite of* our fears about judgement and oblivion. Faith doesn't obliterate fear, but it enables us to live without being paralyzed by fear, and thus to take the practical steps that witness to our hope beyond death. For the person who is able to live in this assurance, for the person who is able to find the grace to go on in the face of fear, for the person who can open their life to the unknown realm beyond death, we have a word: we call that person a person of courage.

And that brings me back to the conversation I had at that hospital bedside some short while ago. The gift of a good death, that last and most precious gift one can give one's family, friends, and society, is fundamentally a witness of *patience* and *courage*. Patience to accept one's powerlessness to change the past, and courage to open one's life to the overwhelming unknown of the future. Patience to live with one's humanity, and courage to face God's divinity. That is what it means to make a final offering of a good death.

And that's why it's so hard to accept that the practice of euthanasia can ever constitute a good death. The irony is that the term euthanasia literally means 'good death'. It's an awful thing to watch a loved one face a slow and painful, perhaps agonizing, decline towards an inevitable but perhaps relatively distant death. Few if any of us would find words to criticize a loved one who looked to a technological escape from a situation of progressive and extreme physical distress and debilitation. But our compassion shouldn't blind us to the fact that there's a genuine difference between passively withholding treatment and active euthanasia.

Continuing treatment, if treatment is no more than delaying the moment of death, serves no purpose. As Arthur Hugh Clough famously puts it, 'Thou shalt not kill but needst not strive, officiously, to keep alive.' But *actively killing*, which is what euthanasia entails, is another matter. Killing those we can't cure and those whose pain we can't ease is an outright rejection of the claims of Paul in Romans chapter 8. Euthanasia is a denial that God is for us and that God is with us. Euthanasia assumes that patience and courage are too much to expect of anybody. Euthanasia is a statement that perpetual oblivion is better than temporary agony. The legacy bequeathed by the practice of euthanasia is a world that has turned life into a disposable commodity, sees memory as a burden and hope as a fantasy, assumes friendship is inadequate and we each die alone, and thus has no particular use for patience or courage, the only virtues that can really give us a good death.

Imagine a society without patience and courage. A society without patience is one that values only what can be had straightaway, searches for technological solutions to every problem, denies the existence of issues that can't be quickly and forcibly resolved, and ends up describing as solutions anything that seems to make the problem go away, even if the solution is worse than the problem. A society without courage has nothing to offer in the face of fear but perpetual distraction, through entertainment, stimulation, or fantasy. It's a society that has left truth and reality behind and headed off in search of something less demanding.

And so a genuinely good death is a gift not just to one's friends and family but to society as a whole. A genuinely good death not only requires and inspires patience and courage on the part of the individual; it requires and inspires a matching patience and courage on the part of family, friends, and society, because it can be a fearful and paralyzing thing to watch a person you love decline, diminish, and quite possibly suffer. If the dying person cannot, for good reasons or bad, find the resources to exhibit patience and courage, their family and friends simply have to supply the shortfall. A genuinely good death is a witness from all parties and to all parties that patience and courage are possible, even in the face of profound sadness, even in the face of crippling fear, even in the face of trying and distressing circumstances. A genuinely good death proclaims that God is for us and God is with us and nothing can ever separate us from the love of God. A genuinely good death is a window into the glory of God, a promise that, in Christ, the future is always bigger than the past, a moment of truth that says, 'What lies ahead is not a threat of obliteration but the gift of completion.' God has given us the assurance of his love and the promise of his presence, whatever happens. Let us resolve to give him in return the most significant witness we can offer: the gift of a good death.

Biographies

Jo Bailey Wells
Jo is Associate Professor of the Practice of Christian Ministry and Bible and Director of Anglican Studies at Duke University. She teaches Old Testament and biblical theology, particularly in relation to its contemporary relevance for ministry. Her scholarly writing focuses on Old  Testament theology. Her books include *God's Holy People: A Theme in Biblical Theology* (2000) and *Isaiah* in the People's Bible Commentary series (2006). Jo is ordained in the Church of England and has previously served as dean of Clare College, Cambridge as well as lecturer in Old Testament at Ridley Hall, Cambridge.

Luke Bretherton
Luke is Senior Lecturer in Theology & Politics and Convenor of the Faith and Public Policy Forum at King's College London. Prior to King's he was Director of Studies of an ordination training course for Anglican,

Methodist and United Reform clergy and before that Research Director of the St Ethelburga's Centre for Reconciliation and Peace. He has also worked with a variety of faith based organisations, mission agencies, and churches in a wide range of cultural contexts both in the UK and internationally, this includes on-going involvement in the work of London Citizens, a broad-based community organization. His books include *Hospitality as Holiness: Christian Witness Amid Moral Diversity* (2006); *Remembering Our Future: Explorations in Deep Church* (2007); and most recently *Christianity & Contemporary Politics: The Conditions and Possibilities of Faithful Witness* (2010).

Steve Chalke

Steve is a UN Special Advisor on Community Action against Human Trafficking and a prominent Christian leader and social activist in the UK. Ordained as a Baptist minister, he is best known as the founder of Oasis Trust, Faithworks, Stop the Traffik and Church.co.uk. Over the last 24 years Oasis has developed into a family of charities now working on five continents and 11 countries around the world, to deliver housing, education, training, youthwork and healthcare. Steve is the author of numerous books and articles as well as a regular presenter and contributor on television and radio programmes. In 2004 he was awarded an MBE for his services to social inclusion by the Queen.

Shane Claiborne

Shane's ministry experience is varied, from a 10-week stint working alongside Mother Teresa in Calcutta, to a year spent serving at Willow Creek Community Church outside Chicago. During the recent war in Iraq, Shane spent three weeks in Baghdad with the Iraq Peace Team. He is also a founding partner of The Simple Way, a faith community in inner city

Philadelphia that has helped
to birth and connect radical
faith communities around the
world. Shane writes and trav-
els extensively speaking about
peacemaking, social justice,
and Jesus. He is featured in
the DVD series "Another
World Is Possible" and is the
author of the several books
including *The Irresistible Revo-*

lution, Jesus for President, and Becoming the Answer to Our Prayers.
He describes his vocation as being a 'Hellfire and damnation
preacher, preacher, writer, and circus performer.'

Stanley Hauerwas
Stanley is Gilbert T. Rowe
Professor of Theological
Ethics at Duke Divinity
School. Prior to Duke he
taught at the University of
Notre Dame. Though he is
often identified as an ethicist,
his work is more properly
described as theology. His
primary intent is to show in

what way theological convictions make no sense unless they
are actually embodied in our lives. To that end, his work
draws on a great range of literatures—from classical, philosophical, and theological texts to contemporary political theory. He also works in medical ethics, issues of war and peace,
and the care of the mentally handicapped. His numerous
books include *A Community of Character* (1981); *The Peaceable
Kingdom: A Primer in Christian Ethics* (1983); *Suffering Presence:
Theological Reflections on Medicine, the Mentally Handicapped,
and the Church* (1986); *Dispatches from the Front: Theological
Engagements with the Secular* (1994); and his 2001 Gifford
Lectures, *With the Grain of the Universe: The Church's Witness
and Natural Theology* (2001). In 2001, *Time* magazine named

Hauerwas 'America's best theologian'. His response? '"Best" is not a theological category.'

Russell Rook

Russell works with Chapel St—a change agency supporting churches and local communities in the delivery of transformational community services. He is also the chair of the Theme Group that develops the core content and curriculum for Spring Harvest, Europe's largest Christian conference. His publications have included two popular commentaries on well-known gospel passages as well as *A Certain Rumour, The Hitchhikers' Guide to the Kingdom*, and, with Stephen Holmes, *Walk This Way* and *What are We Waiting for?*—both for Paternoster's "Thinking Allowed" series.

Samuel Wells

Sam is Dean of Duke University Chapel and Research Professor of Christian Ethics at Duke Divinity School. Prior to Duke he served four parishes as a Church of England priest from 1991-2005. Most of this time was spent in the post-industrial North East and in a socially disadvantaged neighborhood in East Anglia. He also served suburban and urban village communities in Cambridge. From 1998-2003 he was closely involved in establishing a community-led development trust, the first such organization in the East of England. During this time he also launched a non-profit organization working with disadvantaged children. His numerous publications include: Transforming Fate into Destiny (1998); *Improvisation: The*

Drama of Christian Ethics (2004); *God's Companions: Reimagining Christian Ethics* (2006); and *Speaking the Truth: Preaching in a Pluralistic Culture* (2008).

Suggested Further Reading

Introductory

Samuel Wells and Ben Quash, *Introducing Christian Ethics* (Wiley-Blackwell, 2010).

Howard Stone and James Duke, *How to Think Theologically*, 2nd edn (Augsburg Fortress Press, 2006).

Sam Wells, *Improvisation: The Drama of Christian Ethics* (Brazos Press, 2004).

Michael Banner, *Christian Ethics: A Brief History* (Wiley-Blackwell, 2009).

On Hauerwas and Virtue Ethics

Stanley Hauerwas, Michael Cartwright, and John Berkman, eds., *The Hauerwas Reader* (Duke University Press, 2001).

Stanley Hauerwas, *The Peaceable Kingdom: A Primer in Christian Ethics* (Notre Dame: University of Notre Dame Press, 1983).

Stanley Hauerwas and Samuel Wells, eds., *Blackwell Companion to Christian Ethics* (Wily-Blackwell, 2004).

Kelvin Knight, ed., *The MacIntyre Reader* (Polity Press, 1998).